Hearths and Homesteads

Memories and Recollections
from
Sligo Active Retirement Writers

HEARTHS AND HOMESTEADS

Memories and recollections

First Published October 2003
By Sligo Active Retirement Writers
"Martinmount", Carraroe, Sligo

Copyright 2003 © The Authors
ISBN 0 – 9545126-0-X

All rights reserved.   No part of the material may be reproduced or transmitted in any form or by any
means without the written permission of the copyright owners.

Applications for permission should be addressed to the publishers.

Editor: Bernie Doyle
Illustrations: Oisín Ó Gormaile
Photographs courtesy of Eccles Collection, Writers and Friends

This publication has received support from the Heritage Council under the 2003 Publications Grant Scheme

Printed in Ireland by Clódóirí Lurgan Teo. 091-593251

FOREWORD

Hearths and Homesteads is an appropriate title for the collective recollections and comments of a group of senior citizens, from diverse backgrounds, who have lived through the momentous decades that followed Irish Independence. They are part of a fast disappearing age group, which is strategically placed to give firsthand affirmation of ways of life, living conditions, economic situations, hardships, pastimes and relaxation activities relevant to that era.

In contrast to formal documentation used to portray events of the same period of history narrative methods employed by the writers impart a human touch to what were essentially human situations. Perceptions and comments are personal to the writers and do not necessarily conform to conventional records.

The publication is designed to instigate discussion among older age groups who, it is hoped, will be stimulated to recount their own experiences. It will serve also to enlighten younger generations, whose knowledge and understanding of the conditions in which their predecessors lived may be lacking in many respects. In the interests of anonymity, names used in the writings are fictional and should not be construed as referring to any known persons living or dead.

Martin Gormally

The Writers

Jo Butler: Born and reared in Kinawley, Co. Fermanagh, lived in Mayo for thirteen years and has been living in Sligo for more than thirty years. As a member of SARA Writers for the past five years she has contributed to the group's publications: *Evening Echoes* (2000): *Autumn Leaves* (2001) and *Halcyon Days* (2002). She gives recollections of her early life in Fermanagh.

Bernie Gilbride: Born in Sligo town, where she has lived all her life. She started writing in the summer of 2000 and has contributed to *Autumn Leaves* (2001) and *Halcyon Days* (2002). Her other interests include painting and history. Her description of the old buildings and the customs and traditions of Sligo town present a complete contrast to modern Sligo and its environs.

Martin Gormally: Born in the Tuam area of Co. Galway in 1922 and has been living in Sligo for the past thirty-four years. Prior to that he lived in Longford, Meath, Mayo and Donegal. He is a member of SARA Writers since 1997. He has contributed to *Evening Echoes* (2000): *Autumn Leaves* (2001) and *Halcyon Days* (2002). He gives us many varied and detailed descriptions of rural living and farming methods employed in the 1920s and 1930s. He has also provided samples of the remnants of the Irish language, which were still embodied in the vernacular of his youth.

Brigid Gunnigle: Born in Kinlough, Co. Leitrim. Married and living in Castlegal, North Sligo since 1941. She joined SARA Writers in 1997. She was published in *Evening Echoes* (2000): *Autumn Leaves* (2001) and *Halcyon Days* (2002). She has been scribbling on and off for years, and has vivid memories of her youth in Leitrim.

Nora Oates: A native of Grange, Co Sligo, lives at Teesan on the outskirts of Sligo Town. She is a member of SARA Writers since 1997 and has contributed to group publications: *Evening Echoes* (2000): *Autumn Leaves* (2001) and *Halcyon Days* (2002). She tells of rural living in Co. Sligo in her young days.

Mary O'Connor: Born in the Lixnaw district of Co.Kerry in the early 30s. Met and married a Sligo man in England and came back to Sligo in 1964. She joined SARA Writers in 1999. She has contributed to *Autumn Leaves* (2001) and *Halcyon Days* (2002). She loves reading, knitting, meeting people, dancing, playing cards and writing. Her tales are of rural and farming life in Kerry in the 30s and 40s.

HEARTHS AND HOMESTEADS

Sligo Active Retirement Writers

CONTENTS

Western Counties

The Hearth Fire	2
From Scythe to Satellite	4
The Humble Spud	7
As Things Used to be	11
Making a Match	14
Bringing Home the Bride	17
Saving Turf	20
Eviction	23
A Child's Christmas 1928	26
Saving Hay	29
Killing a Pig	33
Politics	34
World War II	36

County Fermanagh

Maytime	42
The Turf Bog	43
My Father's War Effort	46
The Wireless	48

County Galway

Rural Living in the Twenties and Thirties	52
Transport Twenties' Style	59
My May Day	62
Farewell to the Granny	63
Markets	66
The Reek	69

Anglicised Irish in Vernacular Use in
North Galway in the Twenties
and Thirties 74

County Kerry
Christmas and Turkeys 82
Summer Time 83
Our Feathered Friends 85

County Leitrim
Preparing for First Communion 90
Granny 93

County Sligo
Living Conditions Many Years Ago 96
Making the Hay.. 97
Cutting the Turf 99

Sligo Town
The Market Yard in Sligo 102
Games from Long Ago 105
A Townie's Day on the Bog 108
Tobernalt 110
Winter – A Memory 115

WESTERN COUNTIES

*Martin Gormally's memories of his early years
and his lifelong work with the Department of Agriculture
are reflected in his writings.*

THE HEARTH FIRE

Traditional Hearth Fire

'Stay away from the fire' was a constant warning by parents to children who wandered too near to the open fire, while playing or squabbling, in the living room of the family home in an era long past. It was salutary advice in a situation where an unprotected hearth fire was the nerve centre of daily domestic activities. Rural dwelling houses of a century ago contained at most two or three apartments, the largest of which was used for cooking, eating, washing, drying and the myriad of activities that formed a necessary part of family living. A hearth fire, laid at floor level in the chimney recess, provided heat, energy and a measure of comfort for the household. It was synonymous with the word 'home'. Against the rear wall of the broad chimney place a swinging arm of wrought iron was fitted with an array of adjustable crooks, from which cooking utensils were suspended, which were raised and lowered above the fire as required. In an alcove at one side a stone-flagged seat concealed an ash-pit underneath. Replenished from the fuel stack of peat or wood in the yard outside, the hearth fire was never allowed to die. By day it served to cook food for humans, domestic animals and poultry. At dusk, when doors were closed, it provided cosy heat for comfort and relaxation. At night its burning embers were smothered in ashes where they remained dormant and provided the nucleus of the next day's fire.

Soot from the burning fuel accumulated on all artifacts in the chimney place; crane, crooks and flue alike. All demanded regular cleaning. As soot was combustible, the chimney flue had to be cleaned frequently as fire could spread rapidly to the thatched roof. Proprietary flue brushes were unknown to rural people. Instead a stout blackthorn bush, securely fastened midway on a rope, was pulled upwards and downwards until the deposit of soot was detached.

Daytime activities completed, the door was closed and the fireside became a forum for relaxation, dialogue, discussion and storytelling. Womenfolk sewed and knitted as they participated. Neighbours dropped in to *ceilidhe*, some to play cards or music on the long winter nights when few alternative forms of entertainment were available. At the approach of midnight visitors departed to their homes. Rosary beads were taken down and with toes turned to the fire for a final heat night prayers were recited. Before retiring the man of the house covered the embers with ashes, laid a few damp sods of turf on top and placed the tongs lengthways across the hearth as a protection against the evils of the night.

In times of festivity and grief the family livingroom, or kitchen as it was commonly called, doubled as a venue for music, song and dance and sometimes as a place of mourning when circumstances dictated. Here a new bride and her husband were feted on their wedding night, departing emigrants bade tearful farewells and family members were waked. The large deal table, on which successive generations partook of their humble meals, became a stage for step-dancers and solo singers. In different vein it became a bier on which a corpse was laid out in its traditional brown habit while *keeners* raised mournful high-pitched cries as they pinched snuff, drank port and recounted at length the virtues of the deceased.

The hearth fire occupies a favoured place in the Irish psyche. It evokes emotive recollections in those old enough to remember and creates mental pictures among generations at home and abroad, fuelled by stories related by parents and grandparents. Emigrants returning home venerate the toppled ruins of ancestral homesteads and lay bare again the flagstone hearth, the heart of the humble home, where their forebears lived and loved.

FROM SCYTHE TO SATELLITE

As I watched a combine harvester move slowly around a field of golden corn, cutting, threshing, thrusting a cloud of chaff and dust high into the air, and funnelling a stream of grain into an accompanying wagon, I couldn't help thinking of the vast developments that have taken place in farming practice since my early days. I recalled my first job in the harvest field when, at the age of ten, I held a light rod against the standing crop ahead of the mower, to ensure that the ears of corn fell uniformly under the scythe blade into a neat swathe before being lifted and tied into sheaves by older family members.

Harvesting

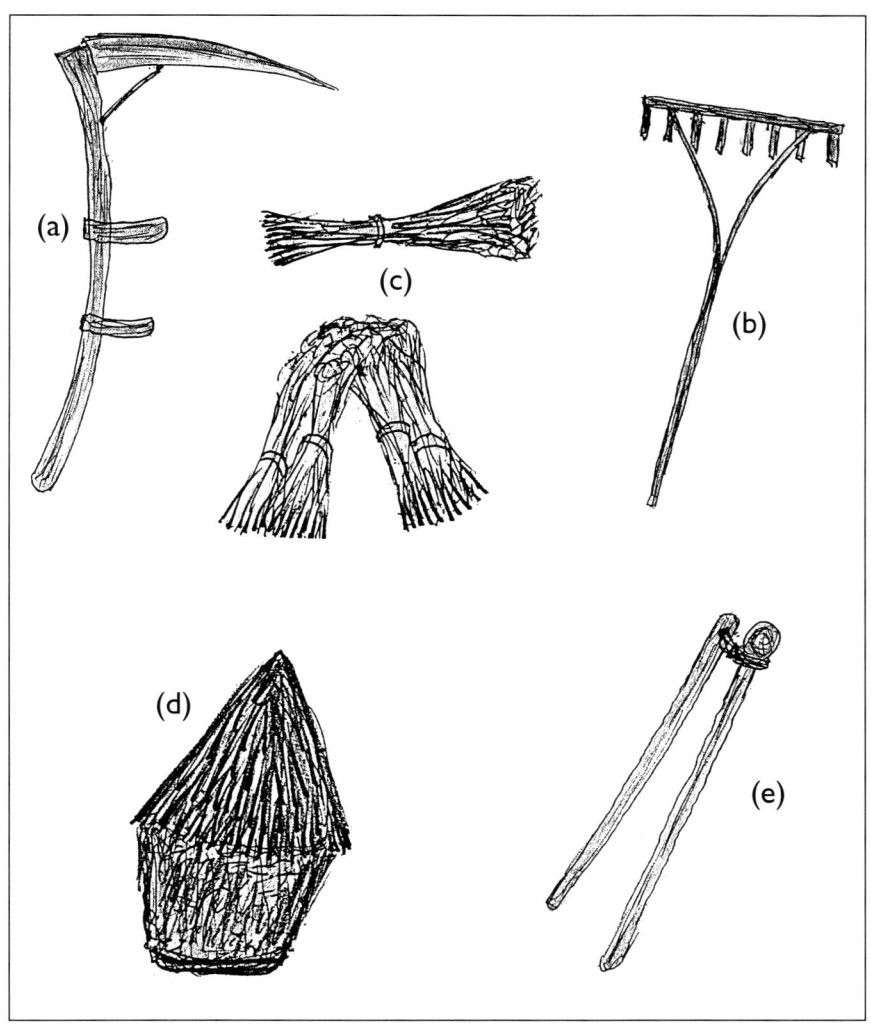

*(a) Scythe (b) Rake (c) Corn sheaves (d) Corn Stack
(e) Threshing Flail*

Mowing with a scythe, lifting the corn, tying it into sheaves and building it into stooks to allow it to dry, were all strenuous, backbreaking tasks on a warm autumn day. Stripped to his waist, his trousers tied with a *sugán* of straw at each knee, the scythesman advanced step by step, his body swaying in rhythm with each wide stroke of the blade as he deposited the corn in neat swathes to his left. Compared with the other helpers mine was a light chore but it was monotonous, and I would have much preferred to gather the luscious blackberries that grew in profusion along the adjacent fences. As I stepped backwards in the sharp stubble my bare feet became scratched and sore, my arms ached with tiredness and I wished that I was old enough to 'take and tie' like the others. How I longed for mowing to cease so that I could rest, but even then there was no release. As evening approached sheaves had to be gathered and set against each other in stooks of eight with two inverted head sheaves to protect the grain. My job was to hold one of these in place while an older member fastened them securely with a band of corn.

As a cutting instrument the scythe had replaced the earlier reaping hook or sickle and was seen as a major advancement in dealing with large areas of corn. Both were soon to be overtaken by mechanical mowing machines in the twenties and thirties. There were two main types: the reaper-binder and the mowing machine. The reaper-binder, in one operation, cut and tied the corn into sheaves and deposited them in the field ready for stooking. The mowing machine was a dual-purpose cutter for meadow or corn. For use with corn it was fitted with a hinged platform from which sheaves were dropped onto the ground ready for tying. Drawn by horses, those inventions took much of the earlier backbreaking work out of harvesting and facilitated cultivation of a greater acreage of oats, barley and wheat.

The decades following World War II saw still further developments in agricultural machinery as tractors replaced horses in farm work and a wide range of new implements became available in parallel with greater traction power. Rotary mowers superseded finger blade versions for the cutting of meadow and silage, while combine harvesters in the cornfield replaced reaper-binders. The *meitheal* of manual workers, so much a part of cutting the corn in my young days, is now no more. The team of two, who operate the combine harvester and trailer wagon don't have to set foot on the field as the golden grain is extracted with speed and precision amid a cloud of chaff and dust. Meanwhile a satellite spy-in-the-sky keeps a watchful eye on the farm below, recording all that takes place for official purposes under EC regulations.

In my youthful days when high walls were erected around big estates to ensure privacy from prying eyes the idea of a satellite spy would have been incomprehensible. I wonder if this and other facets of modern agriculture have now reached their limit or are more still to come?

THE HUMBLE SPUD

When Sir Walter Raleigh brought the first potatoes to Ireland way back in the reign of Elizabeth I, few would have anticipated the momentous influence of his action on our social history. Quickly adopted as a prime source of food for an expanding population, the potato soon became the staple diet of families who were constrained to live as tenants on small acreage. Its potential to produce an enormous crop in undemanding soil conditions, combined with its palatability as a food, made it a firm favourite from the outset. Our people's dependence on the potato for survival became tragically evident when, in the 1840s, it was

Hearths and Homesteads

stricken by a dreadful blight that swept through western European countries. The famine that followed resulted in a population decline of several millions here in Ireland through starvation, disease, death and emigration, all of which has been widely documented. It was one of the saddest periods of our history.

Early Farming Tools

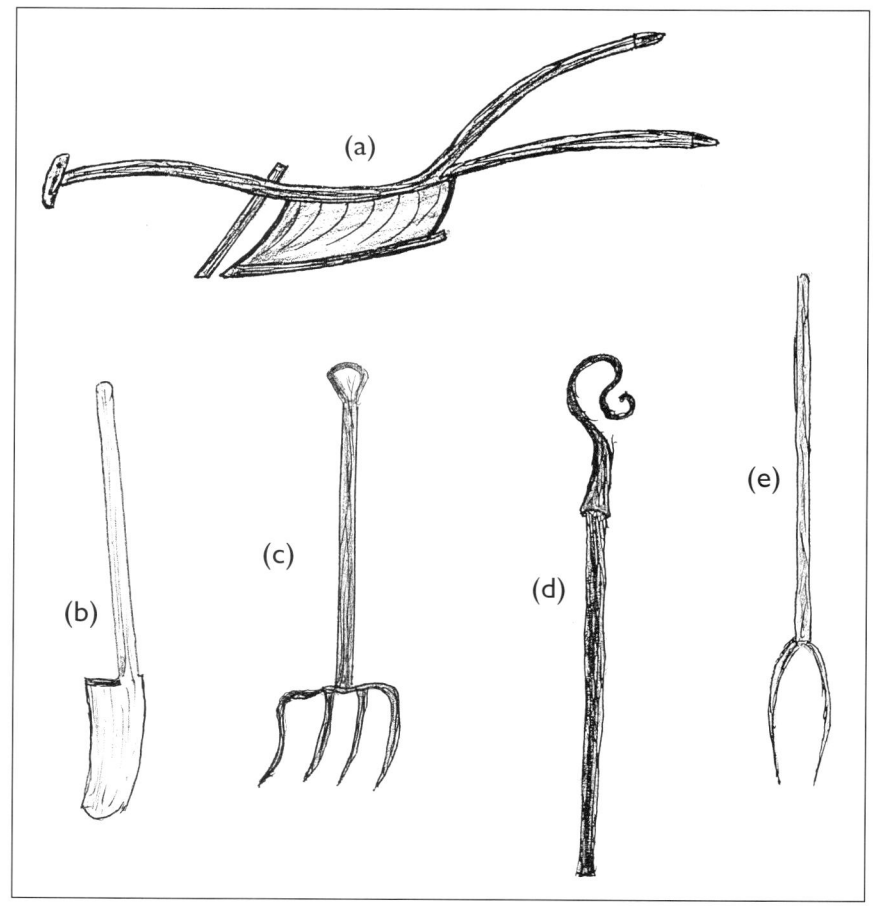

*(a) Plough (b) Spade (c) Graip (d) Shepherd's Crook
(e) Two pronged fork*

I sometimes wonder what sort of potato tubers Raleigh brought to us and if they were called by a particular name. They must have been sweet and floury to have made such an immediate impact. Did they at all resemble the varieties with which I became familiar as a child? By then potatoes had become diversified into a range of different sizes, shapes and colours which matured according to defined categories: first earlies, second earlies and main crop. First earlies ripened from late May to July and included named varieties such as Sharpe's Express, Epicure, Gardenfiller and Duke of York. Among the second earlies that were ready for use in July and August were British Queen and Home Guard. Main crops were the principal line of production and they had an abundance of properly named varieties, among which Champion, Irish Queen, Aran Victory and Golden Wonder were popular. Localised types, usually introduced by migrant workers on their return from farms in Lincolnshire and other counties in England, were also cultivated. These were named after the man who took them home in his suitcase. Other varieties were named after some particular characteristic - 'Defy the Crows' that grew so large that the crow, a noted predator of potato fields, was unable to carry them off, and 'Blight Resisters' which some claimed were resistant to the dreaded blight.

Originally cultivation was done in ridges or lazybeds as they were sometimes called. By turning a sod on each side, a bed of three feet in width was created. The centre of the bed was laid with farmyard manure or dung, the residue from farm animals. Seed consisted of potato tubers cut into pieces called slits, each with a viable bud. Slits were placed at intervals of one foot and the entire ridge was covered with soil from the adjoining alley. When the first new stems began to show a further top up of soil was applied to protect the newly formed tubers from sunlight and predators.

The raised ridge system of cultivation demanded a big input of physical labour, but it had the advantage of producing high yields of potatoes per acre. With the advent of horse-drawn implements and where manual labour was scarce, crops were sown in single drills. Harvesting was done either by digging with spades or lifting by means of a plough until in the thirties spinner type diggers were introduced. Potatoes were stored in a pit in the field, covered with tough heather sods known as *scraws*, followed by straw or rushes and a layer of soil six inches in depth to insulate against frost. Yields varied according to variety and intensity of cultivation, eight to twelve tons per acre being the norm.

Apart from their value as human and animal food, off farm sales of potatoes contributed to the annual income of families in the local situation. In the 1920s a valuable export trade in seed potatoes was developed through which specially selected produce, much sought after in the warm Mediterranean region, was shipped to Spain, Portugal, Malta, Israel, Egypt and the Canary Islands. Under a scheme, initiated by the Irish Department of Agriculture, potato varieties in demand abroad were grown here under strict control at farm level, ensuring purity of type and freedom from disease. When harvested they were graded to prescribed limits of size and marketed in sealed bags bearing details of the contents. Because of our insular situation and disease-free record, Irish seed potatoes established a reputation abroad and were a lucrative source of income for those who grew them on small farms in western counties. With the decline of tillage in those areas in recent years this trade has almost ceased, and in consequence, a valuable export has been lost. The introduction of costly high-tech farm equipment, economically justified only in the context of large-scale cultivation, has resulted in the transfer of potato growing to eastern seaboard counties. Specialised storage of tubers under temperature-controlled conditions allows selection, packing and distribution of table potatoes to be undertaken, irrespective of weather conditions, to any part of the country. Western smallholders, who a few decades ago had a veritable monopoly of growing and marketing potatoes, now purchase their requirements from a local greengrocer. Gone are the days of manual digging, planting, spraying and lifting that those who lived in rural Ireland in the twenties and thirties recall with a degree of nostalgia. Still those with sufficient time and energy to cultivate a kitchen garden proudly proclaim that there's no potato as nice as the one they themselves grow. Who will dare to disagree?

AS THINGS USED TO BE

John Malone was of modest demeanour. He was never a drinking man in the strict sense but when an occasion for celebration occurred he didn't say no to a mild drink. He had lived with his widowed mother until she passed away some twenty-five years earlier. By then he was too old to contemplate marriage and until now he had lived alone in his neat farm cottage. Income from the few cattle and sheep that he reared was ample for his simple tastes. The old age pension that he got at sixty-five was put away for a rainy day that had not yet arrived. Tonight as he celebrated his ninety-fifth birthday he was in a mood to reminisce. Spurred on by his nephew who would inherit John's bit of property, he told us what life was like in the locality when he was young.

'In the late 1800s there were twenty-five families within a half-mile of the crossroads there below. They were tenants of a landlord called Notting and had very small plots of land to live on. The houses they lived in were thatched cabins, mostly of one room, where the whole family had to eat and sleep and there were many children in those days. As the young people grew up they left home as soon as they were able to work. They emigrated to America and never came back. Their parents died and the houses fell in and were levelled. You won't find a trace of many of them now. Some of the better houses survived and the families who lived in them got more land; that's why we have a good few people living around here.'

Ruined Dwelling House

'My father was one of eight children. Two boys died when they were babies. Of the others, three boys and two girls emigrated to America at sixteen and seventeen years of age. They settled there, worked hard and they sent money home regularly to their parents. With the help of that bit of money my father built a stone house. It had three rooms and a *cailleach*. This was a projection in the outside wall, near-hand to the open hearth. The granny slept and rested in it when she wasn't able to work any more. She had a thick mattress of feathers that was cosy and comfortable. A curtain was drawn across to give her privacy and she could keep in touch with all that went on in the kitchen without being in the young woman's way. The *cailleach* was part of most small country houses at that time.'

'There was no electricity or running water and the only heating was from an open fire. Candles gave us what light there was. They were made from rushes steeped in tallow or fat from the animals. Water was drawn from the nearest spring in barrels and buckets. Radio and television hadn't been invented, which was just as well because country people couldn't afford to have them in any case. Food was home grown: potatoes, oats, turnips and cabbage for the house, with any surplus going to feed the hens, ducks, cats and dogs. Hay was saved to feed the cows and horses. People went to the bog to cut and save turf for the fire. Apart from tea, sugar, salt and flour the people were self-sufficient. Barring crop failure or some other calamity they managed to survive. People were generally strong and healthy. They needed to be for there was much hard work – sowing the crops, reaping with a scythe, threshing with a wooden flail, cutting and saving turf on the bog. All of these made heavy demands on a person's strength. There was a job for every hour of daylight. Sunday was a rest day. After early Mass and a big midday meal people often went to bed for a few hours of rest. They deserved it after a week of hard labour.'

'Although life was simple there were occasions for diversion and merriment. Neighbours helped one another and there was a lot of comings and goings between houses. Weddings and christenings were occasions for great celebrations. A musician was always at hand and there was singing and dancing. At the crossroads on summer evenings boys and girls met and danced into the night. In winter there were *ceilidhes* and card games. Telling stories around the hearth fire was a favourite pastime during the long winter nights.'

'All in all I believe that people were more content then than they are today. They may not have had very much of the world's goods but they made their own amusements. Here I am at ninety-five years of age still alive and able to tell the story.'

MAKING A MATCH

If Hubert ever harboured a desire to be married he didn't share his confidence with those near to him. He resided with his ageing mother, an older bachelor brother and an unmarried sister. Together they occupied fifty acres of average quality land on which they grew crops of oats and potatoes and reared cattle, sheep and pigs. They worked as a team. Kate, within the family home, looked after their mother and managed all their domestic needs. Hubert and Dan tilled the soil, herded the stock and provided fuel for the kitchen fire. They were self-sufficient in all but name, wanting only for items of culinary and household requisites that Kate was able to buy with the egg money she got from the travelling shop operator. Their social activities were limited to contacts with their neighbours, Sunday observance and a pint in the local after Mass. Fairs, markets or banking of money occasioned their only visits to town. By comparison with many of the neighbouring households they were regarded as being well off.

After their mother passed away in the spring of 1930, the three remaining members of the household relegated the old thatched house to use as a barn and moved into a newly built dwelling. When the traditional year of mourning had elapsed Hubert's close associates felt that, in the interests of continuity of the family name, it was desirable that one of the brothers should marry. Dan, the elder one, declared his absolute intention of remaining single. He said he would place no obstacle in Hubert's way, even to giving over his entitlement to share the family farm, if that would help the situation. When their brother-in-law Tom delicately introduced the suggestion of marriage Hubert indicated his reluctance to enter the married state. 'I'm rising forty-three years of age,' he said, 'what young woman would consider me for her partner? On top of that I don't know anything about women. I was never out with a girl in my life, and I'd be embarrassed to have to talk to one about marriage. Even if I did meet her, what woman would come into a house with two other family members living there?'

Tom didn't give up. He countered Hubert's objections, diplomatically reassuring him that he was only in his prime, fit and healthy, and that there were plenty of women who would be glad to share his life. As far as his lack of experience with women was concerned he didn't have to worry: his wife would soon fill him in on all he needed to know. And wouldn't the presence of two adult family members be a great asset in helping to run the house and farm? Hubert had a high regard for his brother-in-law, he trusted his judgement and after some more persuasion he agreed, albeit somewhat reluctantly, to think the matter over.

'But how' he asked, 'will I get in touch with a young woman? I don't know anyone well enough and anyhow I'd be ashamed to ask her'. 'Leave that to me,' said Tom, 'I'll put your case confidentially to Fred

Healy the matchmaker. It's many a pair he brought together. We'll see what he comes up with. If you tell me what type of woman you would like, I'll keep a watching brief for you to ensure that the right person is introduced'.

Wheels were set in motion and within a short time Fred returned with a proposition. He had identified a woman, twenty-six years of age, a member of a respectable farming family, who was interested in marriage. Her brother had only recently brought in a new bride and the girl wanted to establish a family of her own with a suitable partner. Hubert felt the blood surging in his veins at the thought of being wed to such a youthful bride. He became enthusiastic, and asked Tom to set up a meeting so that he could see her.

"Not so fast," said Tom, "there are questions that the girl's people will want answered. Her father will question the size of your farm and your title to it. He will want to know what stock you have and whether there are any debts unpaid. He will raise the matter of your brother and sister residing with you and what provision you have made for them. You will have to give him acceptable answers for the amount of dowry that he is willing to give his daughter will depend on these things. When you have formed your mind on these matters I will arrange a meeting."

A venue was fixed, the snug of a neutral pub, where the discussion could take place in confidence. Fred, the matchmaker, was there with the girl's father. Hubert, clean-shaven and dressed in his Sunday best, had a look of prosperity about him. Tom was there to give moral support. After the customary introductions they got down to the business in hand. The girl's father, as anticipated, queried Hubert's credentials and he appeared satisfied that the answers he got tallied with what the matchmaker had told him. The initial sum offered as a dowry was rejected and a spate of haggling, reminiscent of the selling of a beast at a fair, ensued. In an effort to minimise his outlay the father referred to Hubert's age, saying that he would be a pensioner before his daughter had reached middle years. He also demanded a home free from encumbrance for his daughter and a joint sharing of property with her husband. Hubert made it clear that his brother and sister would remain in the family home unless or until they personally decided to relinquish their right to reside there. When the discussion ended in stalemate, Tom suggested that perhaps the girl herself should be allowed to decide the issue, after she had an opportunity of seeing her prospective partner. Meanwhile, could they not agree the question of a dowry? Perceiving the determination of his opposition and fearing a breakdown of negotiations, the father, obviously impressed with the potential advantages of the match for his daughter, relented. A substantial dowry was agreed, a round of drink was ordered by Tom to clinch the deal. The girl, who had been waiting in the wings, was brought in and introduced. She liked what she saw. Hubert, on the other hand, couldn't believe his good fortune. And following some mild celebration the parties went their separate ways. That was the only time the couple met until the day of their marriage.

BRINGING HOME THE BRIDE

It was 1925. I was three years old and not yet conversant with worldly ways. Nevertheless I was aware that something out of the ordinary was about to occur around me. There was a hum of activity as neighbours came together to patch the thatched roof, sweep the street and rebuild gaps in the stone walls that enclosed Peter's house. Womenfolk scrubbed and cleaned the rooms within, painted the table and chairs and put freshly washed curtains on the small square-paned windows. Young boys mixed roast lime with water to whitewash the cart house and byre, and in the process succeeded in covering themselves with lavish splashes of the same material. Everybody appeared to enjoy their self-inflicted labour, calling to one another with lively banter as they went about their various tasks. Finally I plucked up enough courage to ask what the effort was all about.

"Did you not hear?" said Barry, a boy of three times my age, "Peter is getting married next Friday."

Peter was a neighbour and a friend. He was often in our house. I had always considered him an extension of our family. Until now he had lived with his mother, who was old and had recently been unable to do much about the house. Her married daughter, Nell, lived two miles away. While she visited regularly and helped to keep things in reasonable shape, her task was proving too demanding on top of her own domestic responsibilities. She decided that it was time Peter got a woman of his own.

Contacts were made, a willing young woman was identified, negotiations ensued and in due course a date was fixed for the wedding.

At sunrise on Friday Peter with two close confidants, harnessed the mare and set out on the jaunting car. He had to travel twelve miles to collect his prospective bride and take her to the parish church where they were to be wed. Relatives and friends from both families on similar conveyances joined them there. Nuptials completed, all returned to the bride's home where merriment, feasting and drinking went on throughout the entire day. As daylight waned the attendants decided that it was time that the partying should transfer to the groom's place and the revellers, now in high spirits, set out on the *drag* as the cavalcade was called. Bonfires blazing at every crossroads and vantage point along the way conveyed universal goodwill to the newlyweds. Back home young and old waited in muted silence for any sound that might herald their approach. Adults were poised to torch the huge bonfire on the green in front of Peter's house, or to light the suprocks that would be carried on either side of the cavalcade for the final few hundred yards. The sense of excitement and anticipation was palpable as all waited with bated breath for some signal of the impending arrival. I too savoured the atmosphere of the situation. Our vigil was soon rewarded.

Sounds of high-pitched voices and raucous laughter arose on the night air; jarveys cracked their whips urging tired horses to greater speed and sidecars rocked on their springs. Shrieks of fright emanating from ladies, who feared they might be catapulted into space whenever a wheel encountered a pothole, mingled with the cheers of roadside crowds who had gathered to welcome the bride to her new home. As the revellers dismounted and willing helpers took charge of the horses, Peter carried his wife across the threshold, lavishly sprinkled with holy water by his ageing mother. The fiddler in waiting launched into a rousing reel and the rafters resounded to the sounds of music, dancing and laughter as couples took to the floor for the *Siege of Ennis*, the *Walls of Limerick* and *Miss McLeod's Reel*. My older sister took me along to experience the hooley at close quarters. In the crowded melee nobody noticed me but I did get to meet the bride. I thought she looked a little bewildered in the noisy ambience of her new surroundings, but she chatted with me and gave me sweet cake and lemonade. Perhaps she thought I was the only sane person in the company. Unfortunately my visit was cut short when I was taken home to go to bed. Revelling went on until daybreak, I was afterwards told. Next day all was quiet and serene as those who had missed sleep made up for lost hours. Later in the day my mother paid a return visit to establish a good relationship with our new neighbour.

Thus life began for Mary Kate as a bride and a mother, where she and her husband, Peter, lived together in mutual contentment, through times good and bad, for many long years. Having raised a family of three sons and four daughters, Peter departed this life at seventy years of age while she lived to be almost ninety. Theirs was an arranged marriage similar to many of that era. Rarely, however, was there any incidence of disharmony between partners. Divorce was unknown in rural Ireland at that time.

SAVING TURF

Sixty years had gone by since last I travelled that familiar path of the twenties and thirties on the road to the bog, where in summer I helped to cut and save the winter fuel. The recognised requirement was fifty horse-cart loads, to supply our household needs until the next crop was saved. The road, if it could justifiably be so termed at that stage, was no more than a track on the bog surface laid down without any foundation. With the passage of horses, asses and iron-shod cartwheels it became deeply indented with ruts and holes that followed no particular pattern. A wheel sank deeply where the skin of heather became broken, and as the cart regained equilibrium the opposing wheel dug deeper still into the soft underlying peat. Pity the poor man (boy in my case) who tried to steer a safe passage through the mass of ruts at the risk of having the load overturned into an adjoining open drain.

On my infrequent return trips over the years to scenes of my early days I longed to revisit the bog where we had cut and harvested our supply of turf but I was deterred by the memory of that dreadful road. 'My goodness', I thought, 'if I were to drive down there I might never retrieve my car'. Recently in discussion with a local man I learned that a well-surfaced road was now in place and with great alacrity I proceeded to check it out. Today I am back again on the ground that recalls so many memories. I am physically standing on that ground, or should I say what is left of it, for after sixty years of turf cutting the perspective has changed almost beyond recognition. The long line of peat banks that I remember as being relatively close to the road has been pushed back several hundred yards. What used to constitute an immense acreage of uncut bog has dimished almost to elimination.

With nostalgia I gaze across the spectrum of turf face where as many as fifty families gathered in May each year to work on their allotted banks. Strong men, stripped to their waists, delved deeply into the bog carving out heavy sods of wet peat, which they threw from their *sleans* to the waiting wheelers. On flat-bottomed, wooden barrows with wide wheels, the wheelers placed ten, twelve or sometimes fifteen sods and pushed them far outfield to drier spreading ground. It was heavy work. Hands were blackened by the fresh peat and faces were often splattered by bog water. But there was an air of joviality as they called to neighbouring groups who worked on adjoining plots. In the sultry summer air nobody complained about the labour or the muddy conditions. All waited in anticipation for the call to eat which, apart from assuaging hunger, gave an opportunity for rest and relaxation.

No sauces were required to whet the keen appetites generated by fresh air and hard work. Smoke from turf fires drifted gently on the breeze as families boiled a kettle, cooked eggs and sat in the sun to eat. Water boiled on a turf fire gave tea a particular flavour when a whirling wind blew smoke up the spout of a kettle; sixty years on that taste still lingers. Having finished their repast workers, boys and girls alike, rambled to talk and frolic with those of other families, or stretched their limbs before cutting and wheeling recommenced. Despite the tedium of hard work and aching backs, turf cutting was a release from routine domestic and farm occupations and a joyous event to which we looked forward eagerly each year.

As I retrace the steps of my early days I find a scene that has changed utterly: no sleansman at the turf face, no barrow wheelers, no cheery banter or laughter arising from the spreading grounds, no wisping smoke from turf fires. No human sound is to be heard, only the tick-tock of a mechanical digger as it excavates deeply into the turf face and disgorges water-laden sods, to place them in symmetrical lines on the spreading ground. Only the shrill call of a curlew breaks the silence of this now desolate, depopulated place. All has changed. The bog road on which I stand is smooth and well maintained, a benefit to those who use it. Turf is being cut with a minimum of human effort but life as I knew it has gone from the bog. Tom Moore's immortal words spring to mind:
'I feel like one who treads alone, some banquet hall deserted,
Whose lights are fled, whose garlands dead and all but he departed.'

Old Thatched Farmhouse

EVICTION

Bitter famine, dreadful plight,
Blackened fields to left and right.
Corn sold for last year's rent,
Nothing left, all money spent.

Mike and Mary, tenants small
And their children six in all,
Blight has caused their crop to fail
Two in death already laid.

Landlord's agent at the door
'Pay your dues or out you go',
Father, mother plead for time
Room resounds to children's cries.

'What will we do, where can we go?
No house, no food, no future known'.
'Bread in plenty at the Manse,
Take the soup, you have the chance'.

Hearths and Homesteads

'Never, never while we're spared
Will we deny our God above.
He will help us if we trust Him,
Is He not the God of love?'

From the hearth fire rudely lifted
Pots and saucepans thrown outside.
Distraught parents children comfort,
Battering ram already poised.

Neighbours gathering to protest,
Cudgels raised, in anger call.
Crown forces, law and order,
Aim their muskets to forestall.

Bailiff, for your wicked deeds
A day of wrath will surely dawn.
We will seek a safer haven
Where compassion still is known.

Horse cart loaded with their pieces,
Meagre chattels all they own,
Heads bent low, turn their faces
Towards a refuge yet unknown.

Corpses strewn along the roadway,
Death from famine and disease.
Beggars to allay their hunger
In desperation fight and steal.

On the way they pause to whisper
A prayer for those in churchyard laid,
Two young boys brought low by fever,
Who will tend their unmarked grave?

Western Counties

Twelve miles on a haven beckons,
Landlord's house in leafy wood.
'Turn the turf bog into green land
On it you may grow your food'.

On a patch of bog they settled
Mike and Mary glad to stay,
A horse, a cart, a cow, some cattle,
Planted crops, they hoped and prayed.

A modest house – its walls of clay
Stand as sentinels today
To years of toil, new friends found,
And kindly neighbours all around.

Children grew, some chose to wander,
One remained as head of home,
Found a partner close beside him
Reared a family of their own.

Ancestors noble, brave and true,
Through them now I proudly claim
Six generations direct lineage
Of an ancient family name.

Martin Gormally

A CHILD'S CHRISTMAS 1928

'Mama, are you sure that Santa will come tonight?'
'Of course he'll come. Haven't you sent him a letter telling him what you would like?'
'But Mama, do you think he will be able to come down our chimney with his big bag, and will he know which is my stocking? Maybe he'll put my watch in Frank's stocking and then Frank will keep it and I won't have any watch at all'.
'You'll have to trust him. Santa knows each child's stocking. Go to bed now and make sure you're sound asleep when he comes. If he finds a child awake watching out for him he won't come into the house at all. Off with you all now and we'll rake the fire in case he burns his whiskers. Good night, sleep well'.

I had an eerie feeling as I came down to the dark kitchen before anybody else had stirred. Creeping noiselessly through my parent's bedroom I hoped the door wouldn't squeak as I turned the knob. A dim glow from the raked hearth fire was my only guide to where I had suspended my long hand-knit stocking from the mantelpiece. I could identify it by touch from Frank's. It felt full and heavy. Carefully removing it from the nail on which it hung, I emptied its contents on the floor and tried to establish what I had got. Something soft and crunchy felt like sweets, an angular item with wheels must be a wind-up motorcar or train, the long narrow packet was, most likely, pencils and pens and the rolled-up item might be a painting book or a school copy. What, I wondered, was the rounded piece with the knob on the top? Did I really get a watch? With excitement I carefully replaced all in my stocking and not waiting to hang it up again I left it lying on the hearth and silently returned to my bed. Santa had come as promised.

I reawakened to the sonorous sound of my father's voice: 'Christmas morning. Up you get. See if Santa Claus came during the night'. Frank was out of bed like a shot; he was my bigger brother who always went first. I followed at his heels.

'What time is it,' he asked, 'why is everywhere so dark?' He lifted his stocking from its hanger and slowly removed its contents piece by piece, grumbling that he couldn't find the hard rubber ball or the 'Snakes and Ladders' game that he had asked for.

'Will somebody light a candle? I can't rightly see what I got. Why is there no light from the kitchen window? Dad, will you open the front door?' he said. When the door was opened we both saw exactly what we had got. I was happy with my lot but Frank still grumbled. His displeasure was quickly relieved, however, when he looked outside and shouted, 'Look, it's snowing'. We both ran to see across the half-door a veritable carpet of the whitest, powdery snow that we had ever known, so deep that low walls around the street were invisible and the turf reek looked about half as high as it was yesterday.

'Great', he shouted, 'we'll be able to make a snowman'.

'Forget about your snowman for a while,' said Dad as he drew on his heavy leather boots.

'First things first, get yourselves dressed and put on your strong boots. It's almost time for Mass'.

Mass was a priority on Christmas morning. Forget about toys or snowballs for the next hour or two. Dad poked the hot ashes, laid on some dry turf sods and went out to tackle the pony while mother readied herself and the rest of the family. This was one day of the year when we travelled to Mass in the trap. The ceremony was going to be long and there was no question of breakfast until we returned. Fasting from midnight was still mandatory for anybody receiving Holy Communion, and no Catholic worth his or her salt would dream of turning down the Lord's invitation on the commemoration of His birthday. We must be there early to get a seat. Everyone wanted to attend the first Mass so that they would be free to enjoy a long day of feasting and fun. The priest spoke for a long time. I thought the ceremony would never end and I wanted to get back home to play with my new toys. More delays as adults shook hands and wished each other 'Happy Christmas'. Even the pony champed at the bit where she was tethered to a gatepost outside the chapel yard. No release yet as we tramped through the snow to pray at the graves of our grandparents and deceased relatives. Then it was "Home, Dad, and don't spare the pony'.

Snow had ceased to fall but every bush and tree was weighed down, its frost-laden burden glistening in the pale morning sun. Scurrying tracks of wildlife – birds, foxes, rabbits and in some instances their pursuers were clearly visible. A startled blackbird dashed twittering from a roadside thicket to escape the clutches of a prowling cat, while high in the bushes, sparrows and finches awaited the sight of a morsel of food on the white carpet below. We were reminded that we must leave out some crumbs for the small birds when we got home. As we entered the street in front of our house a noisy cackling from the hencoop, a gaggling of geese and quacking of ducks, mingled with the lowing of the cattle in their stalls as all waited for their morning repast. We attended to some of them while Mother was preparing a breakfast of bacon, eggs and sausages, the drifting aroma of which reached us out-of-doors, whetting our already eager appetites. Breakfast over, we donned our oldest, most worn apparel, grabbed a couple of long flat boards and set out for the hill field to set up a sleigh run with our nearest neighbouring children. Weary and fulfilled we dispersed to our respective homes for the big Christmas feast of turkey or goose, followed by plum pudding, sweet cake and lashings of fizzy drinks.

By mid-evening as winter darkness approached, we were glad to remain indoors and play with our games and toys. Nobody, but nobody, would dare to leave his or her own home on the night of Christmas Day; traditionally this was a family night. Tomorrow, St Stephen's Day, was the occasion set apart for visiting friends and relations. When we children had, as was customary, done the rounds of the village from early morning carrying the *wran* and reciting our little rhyme, the pony and trap was again commissioned to bring the family to visit our distant uncles, aunts and cousins. There we recounted how much we had earned from going around with the *wran* and were given more money to boot. Afterwards we were treated to further Christmas fare by generous aunts who went overboard in being kind to us. If we hadn't got sick before we departed we surely did so with the jolting of the trap on the way home. Nobody worried, after all wasn't it Christmas!

SAVING HAY

Haymaking, as it was conventionally known, was one of the principal tasks each year on western farms. A supply of well-saved hay was vital for the provision of winter feeding for livestock. Cattle, sheep and horses all had to be catered for. Adult dry cattle were outwintered and when grass was depleted with the advent of frost in early winter, hay had to be carried to them daily.

Sheep were allowed access to the traditional sheep-cock in which hay had been built around a wooden pole. This prevented the cock from toppling over when it became gutted underneath, and also served to allow a fresh supply to slide downwards when all the hay at the base had been eaten. Cows, younger cattle and horses were housed at night during winter and spring, and hay was fed to them in their respective stalls. In these circumstances pulling, roping and carrying of hay became a routine daily chore.

Haymaking - Thirsty Work?

The more productive grass fields were reserved for hay. All stock was removed from these in early spring and a dressing of artificial fertilisers was given in most instances as soon as growth commenced. Depending on the prevailing weather conditions, the cutting of early meadows began at the end of June and continued at intervals thereafter until September, when late unfertilised meadows had attained sufficient bulk to justify cutting for hay. Methods of cutting advanced from the use of a scythe in the twenties to the horse-drawn mowing machine of the thirties. Tools used in shaking, turning and raking hay also evolved from the two-pronged fork and wooden hand-held rake to the mechanical swathe turner, wheeled hay-rake and horse-operated tumbling rake of later years. These dispensed with much of the manual labour and speeded up the saving process.

Cutting of grass by means of a scythe was a laborious and skilled operation suited only to the fittest. The initial skill involved knowing how to sharpen the curved scythe blade; failure to maintain a keen edge resulted in uneven cutting and greater stress on the operator. The skilled scythesman was a pleasure to observe as, stripped to the waist, trousers tied at the knees with grass ropes, he swung the scythe in a wide arc. Arms, legs and blade were in perfect rhythm as he cut and placed the grass in a series of long swathes three to four feet apart. One acre per day was regarded as a good output. Contrast this with the mowing machine of later years that could dispose of several acres in a similar time.

Successful haymaking was dependent on weather conditions free from rain that in the west of Ireland rarely extended to more than a few days at a time. In the absence of national weather forecasts wise heads relied on particular signs and observations. These ranged from the stage of the lunar cycle to the flight pattern of swallows, the call of the curlew, the sound of a distant train and lastly, but not least, the predictions in *Old Moore's Almanac*. Because of the unpredictable nature of the weather meadows tended to be cut in small lots. Special attention was given to getting the grass dried to a state where it could be raised into small cocks that would tolerate a limited amount of rainfall. These were shaken out again when sunshine allowed for further drying and having been turned over once or twice, the partly-saved hay was made into bigger cocks where it would season for some time before it was made into trams or larger weatherproof cocks. Thus haymaking on each farm continued until all the hay required was saved. Cocks were neatly trimmed and fastened down by means of twisted hay ropes to proof them against wind and rain until the time came for removing them form the field to the haggard.

Transport of hay to the haggard was carried out by building high loads on a farm cart, tying these with strong jute ropes to prevent loss along the way. Building the load was a skilled operation. To achieve a square formation and uniform width of load, rolled bundles of hay were used to create corners each of which was bonded by a further placement on top until an optimum size of load was attained. Flat-bottomed low-slung floats, fitted with winding gears by which an entire cock was hauled aboard by winch, came into use later on large farms, dispensing with the need for loading the hay onto farm carts. Use of these on smaller farms was, however, rare. In situations where the haggard was contiguous to the hayfield cocks were sometimes roped at the bottom and drawn along the ground by a horse.

Within the haggard hay was built into large cocks or ricks, which were neatly trimmed, roped and thatched to protect them from the elements. Proprietary hay barns were a rarity in the twenties and thirties. Removal of hay for feeding of livestock was done by pulling from the cock or by cutting with a specially designed hay knife. The input of manual labour involved in haymaking and the subsequent transport and feeding of the hay was considerable but, in the context of small farms and available family members, it was never an obstacle.

KILLING A PIG

Home-fed pigs provided the principal meat for rural families in my young days. Two pigs were usually killed every year: one in September to provide meat for the winter months, another in March or April to cater for summer needs. To ensure that bacon was edible it was deemed unwise to attempt to cure the meat in any month that didn't have an 'r' in its name. Bacon was versatile in use. Boiling with cabbage was the most common method but it could also be pan-fried or served as roast. Offal arising from carving the carcase together with bone joints, ribs and *grioskeens* served fresh made a tasty dietary variation which became available only when a pig was newly killed. Blood from the pig was mixed with oatmeal, flavoured with onion, salt and spices and cooked to provide delicious black puddings.

Killing a pig was a ritual event that involved the entire neighbourhood. Only an experienced man was entrusted with the task. Neighbours were enlisted to help. After an overnight fast, the loudly protesting pig was caught and tied with stout ropes to the raised body of a farm cart, its head protruding over the edge to facilitate catching the blood in a bucket. A long knife was plunged between the neck bones sufficiently deep to penetrate the heart. If the animal was securely tied all went well and death was rapid, but if the struggling pig broke away there was pandemonium. Stories circulated about one owner who chased his pig around the yard while the knife was still stuck in its throat - afraid to get too close in case he himself got stuck. Having failed to catch the animal, he went for his rifle to shoot it. The pig, when cornered, looked its master straight in the eye, and as he was about to pull the trigger it dropped dead before him.

When the blood was completely drained the carcase was washed in boiling water and scraped clean of hair. Entrails were removed and the pig was suspended by its hind legs from a barn rafter for twenty-four hours to allow for the chilling and firming of the carcase. It was then ready for carving into flitches for curing. Head, backbone, ribs and leg joints were removed and placed in a solution of brine for immediate consumption. Flitches were rubbed hard with coarse salt before being stored in a curing box sandwiched between more salt. The latter process was repeated at intervals of ten days until curing was complete. Later the flitches were suspended on hooks from the kitchen ceiling to dry and to become smoke tainted. The pig's head was sometimes cooked whole to make brawn; more often it acted as a prize to be played for over and over again at card games in rambling houses. Intestines were washed clean, turned inside out, and used as casing in making black puddings. The bladder, when inflated, served as a football for children. *Crubeens* (trotters), spare ribs, fresh pork and black puddings were shared with neighbours who, in turn, reciprocated when their pig was slaughtered.

POLITICS

I was born in 1922 a short time after the new Dáil assembly ratified the Anglo-Irish Treaty. Already civil war had commenced between the forces of the Irish Free State and Irregulars, who rejected the treaty agreement. Both sides were in open warfare with one another and had already perpetrated several atrocities. In an effort to bring the opposing forces into submission a number of their leaders were executed by the Free State authorities. Such measures led to more reprisals and assassinations. The population which, prior to Independence had presented a united front, now became deeply divided between pro-treaty and anti-treaty factions. In some cases members of the same family took opposing sides politically, a situation that continued for many years.

As I reached the age of perception I became aware of deep-seated animosities between neighbours fuelled by aspiring politicians on both sides particularly in the run up to national and local elections. In rural areas the chapel gate after Mass on Sunday provided a forum for electioneering speeches. Some of my most vivid boyhood memories are of two opposing parties endeavouring to capture the attention of the people emerging from the chapel while hecklers from opposing camps shouted one another down and adherents banged on nearby tin roofs to create a disturbance. To me it was good fun to watch but feelings often ran high when listeners taunted one another about their respective affiliations. On Election Day emotions were equally fractious often resulting in brawls especially when the counting of votes had concluded and candidates were declared elected.

Ten years after Independence Fianna Fáil came to power. In an early confrontation with the British Establishment Ireland refused to repay annuities on monies advanced by the British Government under various Land Acts for purchase by tenants of their holdings from local landlords. By way of reprisal the British authorities imposed tariffs on imports of Irish products. Farmers were most severely hit as England was the principal market for cattle, sheep, pigs and dairy produce. This situation, known as The Economic War, continued until 1938 when Britain agreed to rescind the measures. In the interim Irish farming suffered extreme depression. Lack of industrial employment in our slowly developing economy caused widespread poverty and misery. Inadequate diet and poor living accommodation gave rise to much illness among young and old. Health services were not sufficiently organised to cope. Tuberculosis became rampant and entire families were wiped out in some instances.

Farm prices improved substantially in 1939 with the outbreak of World War II. However by then soil fertility was badly depleted, crop returns were below par and a continuing unavailability of sufficient artificial fertilisers added to the problem. In 1949 a major project of land rehabilitation, undertaken by the Government with the help of Marshall Aid, was initiated to remedy the situation but it took many years before the targets set down were achieved.

WORLD WAR II

The outbreak of World War II in September 1939 brought many changes to rural living in the west of Ireland. At first nobody paid much heed as people went about their ordinary tasks assuming that the conflict would be over by Christmas. Wireless apparatus was still a rare commodity; those who had the facility relayed news from the battlefront to neighbours who gathered at night to *ceilidhe*. Lord Haw-Haw's nightly bulletin from Germany was looked forward to with relish as he dished out anti-British propaganda in his customary inimical satire.

By early 1940 supplies of essential goods like tea, coffee, white flour, tobacco and pepper became scarce and imported fertilisers and feeding stuffs were virtually unavailable. Rationing of food items, clothes, footwear, cycle tyres, paraffin oil and candles followed. The use of motor vehicles for purposes other than essential services was prohibited and strict petrol rationing was applied to those under permit. Horse drawn sidecars and traps were brought back into use as the most readily available form of transport. For those lucky enough to have tyres, the bicycle became the standard means of transport.

L.D.F. Group 1943

For fertiliser, farmers were forced to rely on low-grade phosphate mined in Co. Clare and kelp produced from burning seaweed along the western coastline. These were poor substitutes for the imported superphosphates, potash and nitrogen previously in use. Seaweed was used to augment supplies of farmyard manure for growing potatoes and roots, but, in common with grain crops and grass production, yields became drastically reduced and farmers resorted to the purchase of fertilisers on the black market at hugely inflated prices.

The heavy drone of warplanes flying overhead was a common phenomenon as Ireland was in the direct flight path from the American continent to Britain. Many planes crash-landed on Irish soil during the hours of darkness, resulting in most instances in fatalities among the crews. In some cases planes flying by daylight were able to negotiate safe landings which caused a degree of excitement for those living nearby. Fears arose of an impending invasion when parachutists were found to have been dropped in some areas. A call went out from the Taoiseach, Eamon De Valera, for able-bodied men to join an emergency local defence force which would be used as a backup to the regular army in the event of an attack by either of the warring parties. The response was impressive and as a result a Local Defence Force (LDF) unit was formed in every parish. Week by week young men voluntarily gave of their spare time to be formally trained in discipline, drill and the use of arms while older men formed a Local Security Force (LSF) which was designed to assist if necessary in policing. Young women volunteered to train as Red Cross first aid personnel.

Road signs and place names on public buildings were removed; robust timber spikes were placed throughout fields sufficiently large for landing aircraft; roads were blocked at chosen strategic locations; ambush positions were identified, all of which measures were designed to obstruct potential invaders. Rifles, ammunition and bayonets were issued to LDF members, manoeuvres were held in conjunction with the regular army and the force was put on the ready for any eventuality. Life had suddenly become more serious.

As imported food became less available a programme of compulsory tillage was introduced by the Government to ensure national self-sufficiency in essential items. Landholders were compelled to till a stated proportion of their arable land and a quota of acreage under wheat was imposed. Enforcement of these regulations was a heavy imposition on farmers in eastern counties where livestock grazing was the traditional practice and owners were unfamiliar with or unequipped to undertake cultivation. Due to the system of mixed tillage and grass farming practised on small western holdings compliance with the measures was more readily achieved. Wheat for conversion to flour of good baking quality required skilful cultivation and weather conditions at harvest time that, with the vagaries of our Irish climate, were not always attainable. As a result the finished product which became known as 'black bread' was not very digestible and there were complaints from people whose stomachs reacted to it.

Lack of sufficient supplies of coal for industrial and domestic use gave rise to fuel problems in towns and cities. A concerted programme of turf production was undertaken by Bord na Mona on one hand and by County Councils in western and midland counties. Efforts on so many fronts provided a level of much-needed employment as turf harvested on local bogs was transported to Dublin and stacked in the Phoenix Park: a preliminary to distribution to households in the city. Stands of mature deciduous trees in peripheral eastern counties also fell victim to the saw and the axe in an unprecedented market for firewood. Town gas for domestic purposes was severely rationed, supplies were restricted to certain hours, and a 'glimmer man' patrol was introduced to detect covert use of the gas remaining in the distribution grid when supplies were shut off by the gas company.

Service Medals - L.D.F. and L.S.F.

Cities and large towns had the benefits of electric light and power but rural areas did not have electricity for a number of years afterwards. Country dwellers relied on paraffin lamps and candles to provide light. In common with so many other commodities these were severely rationed and did not meet normal requirements. In many homes the glow of the hearth fire was the only light available when stocks of lamp oil ran out. From acquaintance with their local neighbourhood, people became used to finding their way without the aid of artificial light and accidents under this head were rare.

COUNTY FERMANAGH

The reflections of Jo Butler on rural living in Fermanagh around fifty years ago.

MAYTIME

No workman's holiday, no day off school, only primroses on the doorstep ushered in the month of May. Still there was excitement and hope in our outlook as we looked forward to a long bright summer. Green mosses, primroses and violets replaced the brown turf ashes in the school fireplace. The cubbyhole in the cloakroom was swept clean and the few remaining turf sods were herded into a corner. We could drink cold milk from the bottle at lunchtime. Ankle socks revealed skinny white legs and low shoes, sandals or maybe bare feet replaced studded boots. The stepping-stones stood high above the water level as the river floods abated and we could take the short cut to school.

Men headed for the bog. New banks were peeled. White was the prevailing colour – *canawans*, whitethorns, wild cherry blossom and white clover. Little girls dressed in white communion dresses, white waxen wreaths on cobweb veils. Boys were in short knee-length trousers, knees scrubbed clean, smooth hair parted. Lines of washing fluttered – sheets, blankets and counterpanes. Newly whitewashed cottages with whitewashed surrounding flowerbeds, whitewashed buckets of dahlia tubers, white butterflies darting. There were noises everywhere – birds twittering, cocks crowing, calves bleating, cows mooing, bees humming and the cuckoo in the distance.

A memory for me in May was of my first day in school. A new dress, a schoolbag, new faces, white chalk – a new beginning. Starting with a clean slate!

THE TURF BOG

It is a hot afternoon in late May. We get out early from school today. I hurry home. I want to get out of my good clothes. They are not really my best clothes which are reserved for Sunday but my school clothes have to be kept clean as well.

As it is dry weather I can take the short cut through the fields. All winter I have trudged the three-mile journey along the lonely byroad. As I climb over the stile leading into Scale's field I can see the men in the distance. They are in their shirts and trousers and some have caps on. The area around them is black with newly cut turf contrasting with patches of white *canawan*. I put an inch to my step.

My mother is washing the tin can when I get home: it is an empty sweet can that she got from the man with the travelling shop. It used to hold 'Bull's eyes'. I change my clothes hurriedly and fling my shoes and socks under the bed. Oh, the freedom! My mother gives me a thick cut of *fadge* bread spread with salty homemade butter, and I drink a mug of buttermilk to quench my thirst. Then I help her to butter the slices of Farmer's loaf, on which she spreads a generous helping of homemade marrow jam, before sandwiching them together. Having packed the sandwiches and mugs in a basket, my mother takes the boiling kettle off the crook over the fire. She scalds the can before adding a handful of tea and sugar and filling it up nearly to the brim with the boiling water. Enough milk is then added before the tight-fitting lid is secured.

'Off with you now, and be careful crossing the stile, and mind the bog holes,' says my mother as she dispatches me with the basket and the can.

In the Bog

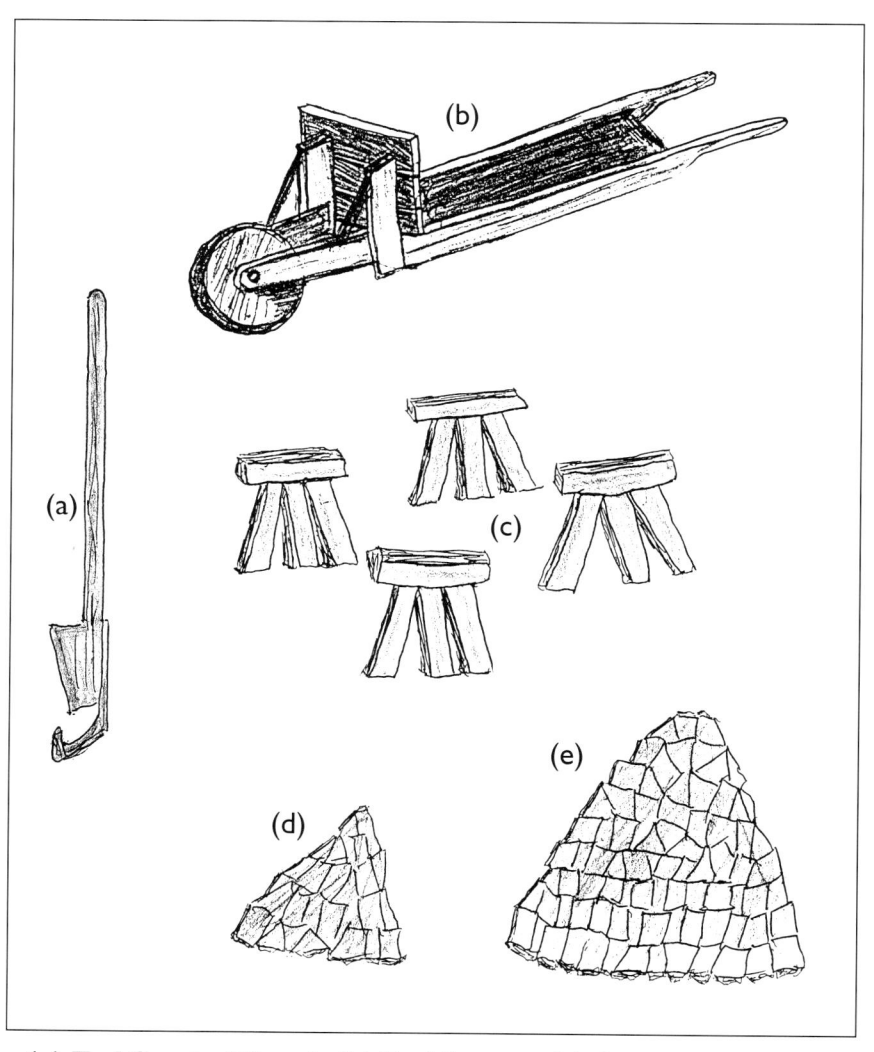

(a) Turf Spade (Slean) (b) Turf Barrow (c) Sods Footed to dry
(d) Clamps (e) Stacked and Saved

I set off across the hill field along the beaten path, leaving down my burden while I open and close the gate leading to the far hill. Here

I follow the newly made path that leads to the bog lane. The grass is softer here and white clover gets entangled in my toes. I am careful crossing the stile and I walk along the cart tracks on the bog lane. Soon I smell the bog. There are small trees with silvery barks growing here as well as the poplars. The leaves on the poplars are moving. My father says that they are always trembling because it was on a poplar tree that Our Lord was crucified. I watch my step now as I could trip on the heather stalks. The men spot me coming and lay down their sleans before planting themselves down on a mound of dry mossy bog. The heather has been flattened out from previous sessions.

'Good girl yourself,' one of them calls out while another asks me how I got on at school today. My father passes around the mugs and, without ceremony, they help themselves to tea and bread.

I run around and find a soft muddy area near the bottom of the bank where they have been cutting the turf. I dance in the soft, velvety bog sediment and feel it squelching between my toes – the water hasn't come in yet to fill up the bog hole. I see another bank that has been freshly cut. The men have spread out the soft wet peat, and have started making indentations in it like squares of chocolate. When these dry the turf thus formed will be called 'muddies'. I shape some of the 'muddies' myself and leave the outline of my hand on some of them. I hope the imprint will still be visible when they are dry.

The men go back to work again and I replace the mugs. There is no tea left in the can. I hang around, pulling the *canawans*, looking at the ants in the heather mounds, chasing the butterflies and sometimes stopping to hear the adult gossip. Eventually my father says, 'Maybe it's time to go home to do your lessons.'

MY FATHER'S WAR EFFORT

It is a piercing cold March day. I have been sent to call the men for their dinner. They are on the far hill field. Johnny is unloading a cartload of farmyard manure. My father is digging ridges in the lea field. He cuts deep into the tough ground and levers up a broad sod with his spade. He has been working like this for several days.

Filling Barrels for Spraying

We are living in County Fermanagh. It is wartime and food is scarce. A letter has come from the Ministry of Agriculture informing my father that he must increase his tillage. All farmers received similar letters. My father has decided to plough the lower hill meadow for corn and prepare the far hill field for potatoes. The far hill hasn't been tilled for many years. Johnny and my grandmother have been sitting in the barn for days cutting the potatoes for seed.

The pieces of potato that haven't got 'eyes' are cast aside and will be boiled for feeding the hens. The segments with 'eyes' have been put in a container with lime.

A cold wind is blowing from the north; my father has his back to the wind. If he faced the other way he could look down the hill, see the green shoots on the lone bush, the winding banks of the Claddagh river, the green slope of Coragh Hill, the shadows flitting over Benaughlin and the smoke rising from the whitewashed houses of Caroo and Mineenbawn. When I call out to my father he shoves his spade deep into the ground, glad of the excuse to pause from his labours and eager to come home for a hot meal. Johnny has already gone ahead with the horse and cart. Tomorrow he will start spreading the manure down the middle of the ridges and when my brother comes home from school he will dibble the potato cuts on top of the manure. My father will then fold over the flaps of soil on either side, and when finished, the ridges will look like long plaits streaming down the hill. His back will ache and he will curse the war but he will be pleased with his achievement.

In May or June my father and Johnny will fill a recycled wine barrel full of blue stone and washing soda and will spray the potato stalks to protect them from blight. It will be autumn when they come back to dig up the crop which will entail many backbreaking hours. The potatoes will be gathered into long heaps, covered with clay and thatched with rushes to keep out the frost and hopefully deter the incursion of rats as well.

My father will wish for an end to the war and a return to his own easy-going methods of farming. All through winter and spring he will enjoy many tasty dinners of cabbage, bacon and delicious floury potatoes.

THE WIRELESS

'I'm buying a wireless,' my father once said.
'That's why there's a wire between the house and the shed'.
Through a hole in the casement all the way from Athlone
The waves they came swirling into our home.

High up on the shelf the wireless was placed,
Wet and dry batteries to its terminals were laced.
A twist of the knob between finger and thumb,
A call for silence, the *ceilidhers* went dumb.

Then out from the wireless trapped waves were set free.
We split our sides laughing at Jimmy O'Dea.
When Joe Linnane questioned the team one by one
We took sides and giggled when the teacher scored none.

We bragged when the farmer came out with top score
And praised him on high for his wealth of lore.
Then Peadar O'Connor used grams of saltpetre
For mending, in times prior to kilo and litre.

We hated the ballads on Saturday night
But Delia Murphy's singing – well that was all right.
Ian Priestly Mitchell was ever so grand,
Bart Bastible sent wishes on sea, air or land.

County Fermanagh

John McCormack, the tenor, sang *Mother Machree*
And *Little Boy Blue* and *The Rose of Tralee*.
The brothers McCusker were always at hand,
They played jigs and reels, such a popular band.

When listening to stories from Barney McCool
'Where's Coolaghy?' says Paddy, 'Go find out at school.'
On Sundays we listened to Micheál O'Hehir
When Kerry beat Cavan or Mayo beat Clare.

Now broadcasts are coming from Montrose, Dublin 4,
We don't hear 2RN or Athlone any more.
I'm a bit sentimental - I don't know about you,
But I still miss the signal *O'Donnell Abu*.

COUNTY GALWAY

Martin Gormally recounts scenes and activities of his early childhood and teenage years in the Tuam district of his native county, Galway, and gives us a flavour of the Irish words then used in everyday conversation.

RURAL LIVING IN THE TWENTIES AND THIRTIES

The centuries-old system of tenants renting land from a landlord had virtually disappeared by the 1920s. Following widespread agitation measures were introduced by the British parliament in the late 1800s to allow tenants to purchase their holdings on the basis of deferred annual repayments. This facility was widely availed of and as a result many farmers became landowners for the first time. A resettlement programme initiated by the British under the aegis of the Congested Districts Board was aimed at creating holdings of a more economic size in western counties. This work was progressed by the Irish Land Commission following Independence and continued until the 1980s.

A Typical Farmhouse

A number of large farms, remnants of undivided former estates, still pertained in Co. Galway but in general holdings of around twenty acres prevailed. The system of mixed tillage and grass farming practised involved cultivation of oats, potatoes and turnips, grazing of cattle and sheep and conservation of hay for winter fodder. On poorer soils rye was grown, while on more fertile land wheat, barley and mangolds were added. Families were large: ten or more children in many cases. There was little off-farm employment; emigration and migration were the only outlets, all of which resulted in an abundance of family labour. Most farm tasks were performed manually and due to the number of mouths to be fed self-sufficiency in human and animal food became the keynote to economic survival.

A Sunday Crossroads Gathering

The typical smallholder family lived in a three-roomed thatched dwelling. Out offices consisted of a cart house, cow byre, pigsty, calf house, barn and sheds for geese, ducks and hens. Indoor wintered livestock were bedded in straw and fed with hay, turnips, potatoes and grain. These contributed to an accumulation of dung which was an essential element of fertilisation in crop production. Potatoes were cultivated by spade labour on ridges three feet in width, the return per acre being greater under this system of planting. Ploughing, harrowing and sowing of corn were done with a team of two horses. Neighbours shared their resources where each kept only one horse. Hay and corn crops were cut by scythe. A wooden flail was used to thresh sheaves of corn on the barn floor. Grain was cleared of chaff and other impurities by winnowing in the open on a windy day. Potatoes and turnips for feeding poultry and pigs were boiled over the kitchen fire before being mixed with crushed oats, barley or rye.

The average complement of stock on a small holding in the twenties might consist of a horse, a donkey, two milch cows, some young cattle, some sheep, a few pigs and a collection of poultry - hens, ducks, geese and turkeys. Basic farm equipment consisted of two carts, one each for the horse and donkey, harness and tackle for both animals, a swing plough, drill plough, a wooden harrow with forged iron spikes, scythe, flail, assorted spades, graips, pitchforks and rakes. The early thirties saw the advent of the spring-tine cultivator, horse-drawn mowing machine, self-binder, mobile thresher and spinner potato digger.

Family members had their respective roles: womenfolk looked after the domestic chores of washing, cleaning, cooking, care of the children, milking cows and feeding poultry and pigs. Men tended the animals and worked in the fields, ploughing, sowing, reaping, saving hay and digging potatoes. Children, when they reached the age of usefulness, helped with weeding, thinning turnips, haymaking, harvesting and potato gathering. Saving turf for winter fuel was a task in which all took part, as well as the chores of drawing water, sheep dipping and bringing livestock and produce to fairs and markets. Every household had a kitchen garden for the production of vegetables and soft fruits: cabbages, early potatoes, rhubarb, gooseberries, apples and currants. Some more enterprising people grew onions, peas, beans, carrots, parsnips and salads while, in exceptional cases, a beehive or two might be found. Initiative and hard work helped families to overcome deprivation, poverty and malnutrition, all of which were prevalent during the depression of the twenties and thirties.

Agriculture

Formal instruction in the practice of agriculture was very much in its infancy in the decade following National Independence. Night classes, given by Department of Agriculture staff when available, were held in rural schools that had to double by day as educational centres for children. Subjects dealt with included crop production, rotation, manures, animal husbandry, livestock breeding, treatment of animal ailments, poultry keeping, egg production and butter making. The list of topics was exhaustive and at best only basic instruction was possible under any head.

In the mixed tillage / grassland farming system practised on limited acreage, maintenance of a high level of soil fertility was imperative for successful crop growth. Farmyard manure was the staple ingredient but this varied in composition depending on the types of animal over wintered indoors and the method of conserving their excrement. Seaweed harvested in coastal districts was used to supplement farmyard manure on inland holdings. A form of artificial fertiliser known as Peruvian Guano was derived from accumulated droppings of nesting birds along the Pacific coastline of South America and became available through local merchants. The decline of landlordism, subdivision of estates and lack of funds and expertise among new landowners, had seriously depleted soil fertility in the decades prior to Independence; much was required to restore equilibrium. Even those who could afford to spend on improving their holdings were reluctant to do so in the light of the depressed prices for farm produce that pertained in the twenties and thirties. Necessary drainage and reclamation were often seriously neglected.

A typical farming year commenced in late autumn when, as weather conditions permitted, stubble from the previous corn crop was ploughed under and left to break down through the action of winter frosts. Ploughing of lea ground was usually postponed until March immediately ahead of sowing a crop of oats. Secondary cultivation of land for planting potatoes and root crops proceeded in April. Fields destined for meadows were closed to livestock at this time and top dressed with Guano to promote growth. A normal rotation consisted of oats, followed by potatoes or roots, with a corn crop (oats, barley or wheat) taken in the third year, followed again by potatoes, roots or green crop. Corn was under sown with a grass seed mixture in the final return to lea.

A lull occurred in cultivation activities when spring planting had been completed. Follow-up works of scuffling, moulding and weeding did not arise for some weeks afterwards. During this interval attention turned to the bog where a supply of turf was cut and spread to dry in preparation for the year ahead. Further work of footing and clamping followed during the summer months before the turf was ready for taking home. On the farm emerging crops had to be kept free from weeds; turnips and mangolds were thinned and as moist summer weather arrived, potato crops had to be sprayed as a protection against blight. July and August were taken up with haymaking and harvesting following which crops were gathered into the haggard in September. Digging and storage of potatoes and pulling of turnips and mangolds were tasks carried out in October by which time the annual cycle was set to start all over again.

The advent of a sugar factory in Tuam in 1934 gave rise to the growing of sugar beet as an extra root crop, harvesting of which continued throughout the winter months. While this involved much hardship in the lifting, crowning and removal of the crop to the roadside under wet soil conditions, it provided a welcome cash return for growers and a source of off-farm employment in the factory for some family members. By-products of the sugar industry, beet pulp and molasses, which were made available to growers, were valuable sources of animal feed. Discarded beet crowns and foliage provided extra fodder for outwintered cattle and sheep.

Diet

For the most part, day-to-day food in the farm home was limited in variety and simple in preparation. Potatoes, vegetables, oatmeal, wheaten meal and meat were home produced. Traditionally, potatoes served with bacon and cabbage or turnip comprised the staple diet of the midday meal. Breakfast consisted of porridge, fried bacon and eggs, with tea, bread and butter. For supper tea and bread and butter were again consumed with eggs or cold meat. By way of variation poultry, rabbits and game birds in season replaced bacon in the diet while herrings and other fish were substituted at the Friday meal.

Two pigs were slaughtered every year, one in autumn, another in spring. Cooking and baking of bread were carried out on the open-hearth fire of turf which also provided the only heat in the livingroom. Pinhead oatmeal porridge, cooked at night and left by the fireside to set, was served with milk and sugar at breakfast. On special occasions roast goose with potato stuffing, or turkey with bread stuffing, were served at the main meal of the day. Potatoes and turnips, stored over winter in clay-covered pits, ensured a sufficiency of supply until the new crops became ready for use in July. As the quality of potatoes deteriorated, due to budding and shrinkage, a special dish called *cally* was created in which boiled potatoes were mashed, beaten to a thick consistency with added milk and scallions and topped with a knob of butter, thus creating a delicious filling repast.

Oats and wheat ground into meal in local mills were stored in huge sacks and kept close to the hearth fire ensuring that all remained dry and sweet throughout the entire year. A proportion of purchased white flour was sometimes mixed with wheaten flour in baking. Dried fruit, raisins, currants, sultanas, caraway seeds and treacle were added to produce sweet bread for special occasions. Eggs were in daily use in the house. The surplus was sold to provide the housewife with ready money for the purchase of tea, sugar, soda, salt and other domestic necessities as well as tobacco for the man of the house.

Two sets of family clothes were maintained: one for best wear to Sunday mass and special outings, another for daily work around the farm. Corduroy trousers and frieze greatcoats were commonly worn by the men while much of the apparel of women and children consisted of home knit jumpers and cardigans. Stout leather boots topped by leather leggings provided a measure of waterproof outdoor wear in an age when rubber wellingtons were unknown. Wooden-soled clogs, warm and light, were popular with children. Grown men wore what were familiarly referred to as 'nailed boots' of heavy leather, the soles of which were covered in steel studs and heels fitted with steel tips.

Sports and Pastimes
Outings were limited to attendance at Sunday services, fairs and markets, with an occasional trip to the nearest town or a visit to

relatives. As Sunday was a day of rest only essential domestic or farm chores were undertaken and this became a favourite time for sport or relaxation. Games of football or hurling were exclusive to Sunday - also athletics, bowling, local patterns and fetes. On Sunday evenings in summer, crossroads dances provided a congenial outlet for young people and an opportunity for boys and girls to get together. Traditional music was very much alive in rural areas and there was never a dearth of performers.

During winter months outdoor activities ceased with the onset of darkness. Rural electrification was yet two decades away. Wireless broadcasting was relatively new and very few homes had a receiving set. Neighbours gathered in each others houses where fireside conversation and storytelling helped to pass many a long night. Some played cards for stakes of money, pigs' heads or turkeys. Children with improvised toys entertained themselves. Light that emanated from an oil lamp or candle was rarely strong enough to permit reading. Playing pranks on susceptible people, notably aged people living alone, was a favourite pastime for some mischievous young boys. While tricks were irritating for the victims, apart from the inconvenience caused, no major harm resulted and all was taken in good parts.

TRANSPORT – TWENTIES STYLE

Viewed from today's perspective of multi-transport facilities, the position that applied in rural Ireland in the twenties was extremely basic. Prior to the construction of a national network of railways and canals, transport and travel was best served by the humble horse. Nobles in their gilded carriages, the post-chaise outfit drawn by teams of two or four horses, the undertaker seated high on his glass-bodied hearse, the jarvey on his jaunting car, the carter and smallholder in his horse-drawn cart and the solitary mounted rider, all depended for transport on the strength, agility and persistence of man's faithful, four-legged friend.

Canals and railways of the late 1800s provided an organised transport infrastructure between principal cities and towns from which roads, insofar as these existed, radiated into the hinterlands beyond to more isolated smaller centres of population. Carriage of goods and passengers to and from canal depots and railheads became thereafter a feature of everyday rural life and developed into a way of living for enterprising persons.

Growing up in the twenties alongside the main road artery between Galway and Sligo, I got a bird's-eye view of traffic on that route. Although motorised transport had made its debut on some Irish roads twenty years previously, only three such vehicles used this route on a regular basis. A mail van brought the post to rural post offices, a passenger car plied daily between Dunmore and Tuam conveying travellers to and from the railway station and a huge steam lorry on solid rubber-shod wheels carried heavy goods from the railhead to shops and stores throughout north Galway. The alternative means of transporting goods was by horse and cart, whose owners frequently made a living from carrying light items for hire. Consignments of foodstuffs, tea, sugar, drink, meal and flour were conveyed daily with hardware items such as tools, blue stone, washing soda and animal medicines from the railhead to country shops and public houses as far distant as twenty miles. Charges for such services were mutually agreed between the consignee and carter, payment often being by way of barter for household or farm commodities.

A rather unique facet of transport in that era was the carriage of pigs from monthly fairs at Dunmore, Glenamaddy and Williamstown, to the railhead at Tuam for consignment onward to bacon factories and points of export. Pig buyers at each fair hired carters for the job and only those who were already well known and trusted were employed. As pigs were of heavy weight and liable to become fractious when confined in close quarters, carts had to be fitted with strong cribs at least three-and-a-half feet in height. Each cart accommodated between five and seven animals depending on their size. Adult pigs were prone to fight with each other, often inflicting serious bleeding and bodily damage. Each carter was obliged to carry a long-bladed butcher's knife. If an animal incurred significant loss of blood or succumbed to overcrowding in the cart, the hirer instructed that the pig should be killed outright and suspended vertically by its hind legs in order that bleeding of the carcase would be complete. It was common to see a cart passing by with one or two carcases hanging from the crib. The carter had to be continually on the alert for trouble until he had delivered his load; otherwise his future employment was put at risk.

Carters of porter and general merchandise had an easier run. Seated on top of their cargo they were free to view the countryside and to dialogue with those they met on the way. At the various delivery points the consignee often treated them to food and drink in return for other messages carried for him on the side. On a thirsty day unscrupulous carters were known to extract a free drink from a keg of porter by boring a small hole through the bung, inserting a goose quill, and sucking some of the contents. When satisfied, a matchstick carefully pared to fit was inserted to plug the hole. The publican had no way of checking and would be unaware of his loss unless he noticed a major discrepancy in the weight of the keg.

By the end of the twenties motor cars, petrol driven lorries and vans fitted with pneumatic tyres gradually appeared on the road, shrouded in clouds of dust as their speeds increased. Later a tar-based surface was applied by which time privately owned vehicles had become more common. The progress of transport thereafter is a matter of history.

MY MAY DAY

May 10 was an important date in the place where I grew up; it was the monthly fair day in the town of Tuam. On May 10, 1926 I was much too young to go to the fair. Alas, I was not considered too young to start school. At three-and-a-half years of age, the youngest of six, I was very much the baby of our family. Normally I would have gone to school at five. Why then, you may ask, did my parents send me at three-and-a-half? In our three-teacher school the ratio of pupils per teacher had dropped and the job of the junior teacher was on the line. As a result parents were asked to send along any child fit to walk in order to swell the numbers on the roll. Thus began the saga of my early education. By way of consolation I wasn't the only one deprived – some pupils arrived complete with feeding bottle and teat.

I don't recall any tearful parting from my mother. I feel sure she felt anguished at seeing the last of her fledglings leave the nest but kept a brave face for my sake. Unwillingly, in the care of my older sister, I was hustled away to join the queue of scholars who passed our gate each morning. In common with others I was barefoot. No self-respecting boy would tolerate footwear from the beginning of May until the advent of the first winter frosts. The mile long dirt road had lots of sharp stones hidden from view under the dusty surface that gave rise to bruised feet and broken toes as summer went by.

That road remains indelibly imprinted on my mind to this day. On my first journey it seemed unending. Thoughts of being confined in a classroom for hours on end weighed heavily on my mind as did stories that I had heard of teachers who lashed out with a big stick when an unfortunate pupil incurred their wrath.

I didn't suffer any such abuse on my first day. I am sure the teacher was so pleased at the increase in class numbers that she kept the cane under wraps. Every morning she cycled three miles to school and took along her midday repast. On this day she evidently fancied bananas for lunch but the shopkeeper popped a bad one in her bag when she wasn't looking. As I sat among the girls beside my sister I was graciously presented with a long black-looking object. Never having seen a banana before I examined it carefully and squeezed it a few times before proceeding to demolish it, skin and all. The mess on my face gave rise to giggles from the girls around me and in stern tones my sister was instructed to take me outside and clean me up. The sense of shame that I experienced from being ridiculed in front of my peers on my first day at school left an indelible mark. It was but a foretaste of many indignities that I suffered at the hands of the same teacher during several years spent in the lower classes. What a reward! She was the person whose job I helped to save by starting school at three years of age. Moving to a higher class at seven I escaped from her clutches. Hallelujah! That was my real May Day.

FAREWELL TO THE GRANNY

The granny, my father's mother, lived in a separate apartment that constituted the southern end of our long thatched house. It had its own entrance and there she resided with her husband who died in 1922. My earliest recollections were of a formidable old woman dressed in a red petticoat, black blouse and white *binneog* (headsquare). She was of an independent disposition, kept mostly to herself, and though she talked to us as children, we rarely entered beyond the door of her sanctum. Without being told, I gathered that she didn't approve of my mother and made no secret of the fact which explained why the house was subdivided to allow both parties to live independently of each other. Two members of her family, my uncle and aunt, lived near at hand and visited her from time to time. Three other daughters had emigrated to America where they remained for the rest of their lives.

I recall as we gathered around the hearth fire one dark winter night there was a knock on the door, the latch was lifted, Granny appeared on the doorstep and announced dramatically, 'I am coming in to die'. My mother and father took her in, gently laid her down on a folding bed in the warmth of the kitchen fire, and immediately sent for the doctor and the priest. She was ill for a few days until, as she had predicted, she quietly passed away at seventy-five years of age. The year was 1927. She had been born in the aftermath of the Great Famine and had lived through the Fenian Rising, the Land War, the Boer War, the 1916 Rising, World War I and Irish Independence.

Granny's wake and funeral made a lasting impression on my young mind. Although I was little more than four years old I was already at school and was able to absorb much of what went on. The corpse was laid out in our best room, dressed in the traditional brown habit of that time. A table by the bedside, covered in a clean white cloth, held two lighted blessed candles, a crucifix, a cruet of holy water and a sprinkler. Some neighbouring women of the granny's vintage sat on our best chairs around the bed, speaking in low tones as they drank tea and port wine and extolled the virtues of the deceased. Nobody would dream of speaking ill of the dead. Snuff, tobacco and *dúidíns (*clay pipes) were laid on a table in the livingroom for anyone who wished to partake. In the cart house across the street, swept clean in advance, a barrel of Guinness was set on a trestle and the black stuff was dispensed to all comers. Neighbours, relatives and well-wishers chatted with one another in the kitchen or took short trips outside to relieve congestion when the room became overcrowded. Most went home at midnight but some close friends remained to sit with the corpse through the night.

From early on the following morning relatives and mourners began to arrive on horseback or sidecar to pay their respects to the deceased and to attend her removal. Neighbouring women helped in dispensing tea, scones, wine and soft drinks. My father treated long distance travellers to whiskey. Porter continued to be served in the cart house. As traditional hospitality was dispensed in memory of the granny, the smell of tobacco smoke, alcohol and snuff that permeated the entire house made me sick and I remained outside most of the time.

By mid-afternoon the undertaker arrived riding high on a horse-drawn glass hearse with a yellow coffin inside. Resplendent in his long black coat, starched white collar and hard black hat tied with a white ribbon, he resembled in my mind a character often described to us in fireside ghost stories. Two black horses, the polished brass buckles of their harness shining in the pale winter sunlight, appeared equally weird as they drew up alongside the door of our house. The coffin was removed from its glass shrine and taken indoors. People emerged to allow the remains to be placed inside and with my brothers and sister I was called to say goodbye to the granny before the lid was fastened. The coffin was replaced in the hearse and soon the cortege moved away in the direction of Cortoon chapel. Family members and mourners followed in sidecars, in traps and on foot. Every door en route was closed out of respect for the deceased as the funeral procession went by. High Mass next morning was followed by interment in our family plot in the adjoining cemetery, where a monument in memory of those who had died before her stood. Burial completed, prayers were recited by the priest and the mourners slowly adjourned to the nearby hostelry for a farewell drink before going their respective ways.

The granny was dead. I was sad as I entered her apartment; a presence was missing. Soon after a doorway between our room and hers was reopened and the house was restored to its original purpose as a home for one family. It provided much needed extra space for all.

MARKETS

The cold grey sky of a winter morning, frosty fog glistening on every leaf and icicles hanging from branches, signalled a sharp dry day ahead. Before the sun had yet begun to thrust its feeble rays above the eastern horizon a flurry of activity could be heard on roads leading to the town of Tuam. Early risers urged horses and donkeys to a faster pace in a race to be first on the Square for the weekly market. Sacks of potatoes and oats had been carefully prepared and loaded onto carts the previous day. Square-built cartloads of hay and straw tied tightly with strong ropes, heaped cribs of turnips and turf, donkey carts laden with cabbage, carrots and parsnips lay ready awaiting transportation. Chickens, ducks and geese, tied together in pairs by their legs, quacked and squawked as they were taken from their night shelters. Bonhams squealed as they were lifted from their warm beds and deposited in a canvas-covered cart. All were destined for their respective stands at the Saturday market.

Beside the ancient high cross and its protective railings stood the market house with its platform weighbridge, where cartloads of hay, straw and turnips were weighed after a sale had been negotiated. On the Square alongside was a huge tripod with two swinging decks on which sacks of oats and potatoes were balanced by 56lb., 28lb., 14lb., 7lb., and smaller iron weights.

At Butler's corner town housewives purchased their requirements of fresh vegetables, while under the Town Hall clock countrywomen sold their chickens, ducks and geese, all struggling on the street surface and flapping their wings in an attempt to escape. At the adjacent corner a fishmonger loudly advertised his herrings. Further out on High Street suck calves and young pigs vied with each other for space and sound. In a vacant area a street seller displayed an array of delph, glassware, ornaments, tools and household utensils, while yet another sold second-hand clothes and shoes at knockdown prices.

Sellers and buyers went through the usual to-ing and fro-ing in an effort to gain advantage; the seller asking more than he expected to get, the buyer bidding less than the item's value. Following a spate of haggling a compromise was reached, each party believing that they had come out best in the deal. Produce was weighed, money changed hands and both sides were happy. The principal obstacle was oversupply when buyers took advantage of the situation and sellers were faced with either selling at a poor price or taking goods back home, something that nobody quite liked to do. Town-based traders usually mopped up what was left on their own terms, knowing that country folk needed cash in hand to purchase domestic requirements for the week ahead.

The biggest market of the year took place on the Saturday prior to Christmas, traditionally known as *Margadh Mór na Nollag*. Street space around the Square on that day was inadequate and sales of turkeys and other fowl were transferred to The Shambles, an enclosed yard on Vicar Street. Irrespective of prices obtained for produce, an atmosphere of gaiety and goodwill pervaded the town on Christmas Market Day. There was an occasional flit to the nearest hostelry for a warm-up when bargains were clenched – the spirit of Christmas ruled supreme.

Apart from disposing of their produce, country people had two other items on their agenda that day. The first was shopping (buying the Christmas) as it was called, the second item was going to confession in the anonymity of the Cathedral where they felt more at ease than in their local parish. In appreciation of their support throughout the year, every family grocer donated a Christmas box to his customers. This practice gave rise to much comparison among housewives who tried to determine which was the best place to shop. A pound of best tea, half a stone of sugar, a bottle of port wine, an iced cake, together with a jug or teapot filled with jam, might constitute a hamper for best customers. Less prolific spenders had to accept less. Children accompanying their parents were treated to lavish helpings of biscuits and lemonade. Wise grocers knew that the way to grownup hearts was through their children.

On the day of the Christmas market my greatest joy as a child was to pay a visit to John Waldron's toyshop. There, with face glued to the window and hand coupling the half-crown in my pocket, I coveted every colourful ball, motor car and train set and deliberated on which one I would purchase now that Santa Claus had eliminated me from his list. As evening began to close it was time to set out for home. Everybody was happy and fulfilled with the day's undertakings, secure in the knowledge that Christmas was but a few days away and that all was well.

THE REEK

Town centres in Ireland are called by a variety of names such as The Square, The Diamond, The Triangle or The Mall. The Octagon in Westport, Co. Mayo, is a fitting description for a carefully planned centre from the corners of which roads fan out to the hinterlands beyond. On one of those wet and windy days so frequently encountered in the west of Ireland, I sheltered beneath the awning of a butcher's shop and looked again across the now deserted streets with which I had first become acquainted more than sixty years ago. In the mist-laden background I could just about identify the conical outline of Croagh Patrick silhouetted against a darkening western sky. The scene brought to mind the many times when, accompanied by boys and girls of my youthful years, I set out from my home town of Tuam on the annual pilgrimage to The Reek. Down the street from where I stood was a café – I felt sure the location was still the same – where before twelve o'clock on that Saturday night we partook of our final collation of the day. Fasting from midnight was obligatory for anyone who wished to receive the Eucharist. In my mind's eye I saw again the array of bicycles thrown higgledy-piggledy around the Octagon, each with its stout stick tied to the crossbar and a bundle tucked under the spring-loaded carrier. On the occasion of the annual pilgrimage, the last Sunday of July, Westport resembled to my mind all that I had read about the Klondike during the early years of the gold rush. The Octagon was awash with people coming and going; doors remained open, licensing laws were ignored or waived, eating establishments churned out huge plates of bacon, eggs and sausages to hungry pilgrims. The sweet aroma of food and drink raised the spirits of people as, in the dim half-light, they loudly greeted friends they hadn't seen since the previous year.

Croagh Patrick - The Profile

For me it had all started on the previous Saturday evening in Tuam. For a week before Garland Sunday, the traditional day for climbing The Reek, the question circulating among us teenagers was, 'Are you coming to The Reek this year?' All readily assented with the proviso, 'I hope I can get the loan of a bike.' I won't pretend that our motivation was entirely spiritual. Perhaps it was more an opportunity to be together for twelve hours free from parental observation. It also presented a challenge to our physical ability to cycle fifty odd miles there and back and climb the mountain in record time. One hour and three-quarters for the ascent and half an hour less for descent was our target. As the summer sun began to sink below the horizon we set out in two's and three's on the road that led through Castlegrove, Kilmaine and Ballinrobe, bearing left at Partry on the long run into Westport. Barring punctures or other delays, we allowed three hours to be there by eleven-thirty. Having eaten and stretched our limbs we continued in darkness for the final four miles to Murrisk. A few storm lanterns hanging within the hastily erected tents that sold rosary beads, medals and St Patrick badges, cast a limited illumination as we dumped our bicycles, donned our oldest clothing and boots and carefully folded our best things under the spring carriers. There was no question of anything being locked. Nobody would dream of stealing at the foot of The Reek.

We looked at the bulk of mountain towering two-and-a-half thousand feet above, where a tortuous path was dotted with a myriad of torchlights, carried by more prudent pilgrims. As we started on the soggy path we were glad they had such foresight. Our boots were already squelching from having, in the dark, walked into several water holes. The first half-mile was easy going and with youthful energy we passed more sedate walkers with cryptic comments about their lack of speed. Past the statue of St

Patrick the climb became steeper and we were forced to stop from time to time as some member of our group became winded. A flow of genial conversation and goodwill emanated from the climbers, those experiencing difficulty were helped along patiently by others. It didn't matter whether or not people knew one another; all were united in one common undertaking – getting safely to the summit. On the upper part of the mountain the gradient was so steep that climbers had to lean forward to prevent overbalancing. A glance over the unprotected ledge was enough to scare the most foolhardy. Loose shale shifting under every step added to the need for care as this steepest part of the slope was negotiated. In the rarefied air breathing became difficult and frequent stops were required. 'Not to worry', we said, 'we're almost there.'

The scene at the top was bizarre. A feathery mist enveloped the tiny oratory, its doors locked tightly awaiting the arrival of the Archbishop, who would celebrate Mass there at dawn. In the gloomy half-light young and old milled around the traditional station beds reciting the rosary, many on their knees or walking barefoot through the roughly strewn stones and mud. At points along the perimeter of the crowd local residents tended smoky turf fires and plied their trade of selling cups of tea at exorbitant prices. If a customer complained it was pointed out, without apology, that water and other provisions had to be transported from Murrisk on the backs of donkeys and this was the only occasion during the year when the suppliers could make a few pounds. Nobody really minded. We youngsters had no need for tea - in any case, it was never hot, as the water wasn't properly boiled.

Climbing the Reek - The Ascent

Pilgrims arrived at the summit of the mountain in such vast numbers that movement around the stations became more and more difficult. We took advantage of the situation by hastily reciting a few prayers and starting on our descent. By this time dawn had arrived and a morning sun dissipated the mist, leaving the mountain in stark perspective for those who chose to climb in daylight. Due to the volume of people climbing and descending the narrow path became congested and greater care was called for, particularly by those coming down, in order to refrain from running and to avoid going headlong down the mountainside. 'How far more is it to the top?' was the frequent question from sweating, weary, first-time pilgrims as they gazed apprehensively at the steep path ahead. Consolingly we told them that it was not very far; reassured they plodded onwards. Not everyone was fortunate enough to realise his or her ambition. Sprained ankles, grazed knees and broken limbs were regular occurrences and ambulance crews were kept busy carrying victims of misadventure safely to the bottom.

Weather conditions were always unpredictable and as often as not it rained on Garland Sunday. If however we were favoured with sunshine and clear skies the view from The Reek was a reward in itself. Clew Bay, with its hundred little satellite islands stretching out below, appeared as if it were tilting upwards to meet us. In the distance fishing boats looked like crumbs on a tablecloth. We landlubbers stopped to gaze with awe on the magnificent panorama and regretted that we hadn't been born near the sea. Back to reality we completed our descent, found a sheltering bush under which we changed clothes, retrieved our bikes and set out on the long road home. Despite weariness and lack of sleep all remained in high spirits until at 10 o'clock on Sunday morning we wheeled in home, ate a hearty breakfast, and retired to bed for an eight hour sleep. By then it was time to go dancing. We talked at length about our pilgrimage and vowed we'd climb The Reek again next year.

ANGLISED IRISH IN COMMON USE IN NORTH GALWAY IN THE 1920S AND 30S.

People born in my native Cortoon up to the time of the Great Famine of 1845-7 spoke Irish habitually. One generation later their children didn't understand the language. The Primary Education system of the 1800s positively discriminated against Irish. A tally stick hanging around each pupil's neck had a notch cut for every time an Irish word or expression was used and punishment was meted out accordingly.

When I started school in 1926 a more nationalistic approach had come about. The language was then promoted with the same diligence as those earlier efforts to efface it. This presented a problem for teachers who weren't very conversant with the language and pupils who were compelled, in some instances rather forcibly, to learn it. In company with my peers I bore the brunt of enforced teaching. I had no fallback; my parents were unable to help me. Despite those difficulties I developed an affiliation with Irish and a love of the language that has remained constant throughout my life.

As I grew older I realised that many words and phrases in common everyday use in my native area were of Gaelic derivation, inherited from previous native speaking generations. Local place-names, anglicised by Establishment Authorities over centuries of occupation were, in many instances, distinctly Irish in origin. Prefixes such as Carrow (*Ceathrú*), as in Carrowreagh, Carrowpadden, Carrowkeel; Knock (*Cnoc*), Knockatea, Knockavanny; Kill (*Cill),* Kilconly, Kilbannon, Kilclooney; Cloon (*Cluain*), Cloonmore, Cloonarkin, Cloontoo, which frequently arose are but a few examples. Similarly words and phrases that we used in everyday conversation were Irish although at the time we didn't realise their significance. To give but a few instances, boreen (*bothairín*), colleen (*cailín*), crooskeen (*cruiscín*), gowlogue (*gabhlóg*), binnogue (*binneóg*), were normal in the vernacular. We never stopped to think what their equivalents in English might be.

The extent to which Irish words and phrases were used in rural areas was exhaustive. Within the family home the chimney might be a puthogue (*putóg*), embers on the hearth were greesach (*gríosach*), the old woman was a callagh (*cailleach*), the bed in the alcove in the livingroom was named after her. She slept there at night and during the day she might sit on a soogawn (*súgán*) chair. Her misshapen foot was a spawge (*spág*). Granda's pipe was a doodeen (*dúidín*), the drip from it was sooder (*súdar*), and a drip from his mouth was a pishleen (*pislín*). If he liked a drop of whiskey he was given a theesgawn (*taoscán*); if he had a beard it was a feasog (*féasóg*). If some of his front teeth were missing he was montaugh (*manntach*). If a man was a good storyteller he was a shanachee (*seanachaidhe*); if he indulged in silly conversation he was talking ramesh (*ráiméis*); if he had a few drinks too many he was magalore (*maith-go-leor*) or he had been on a spree (*spraoi*). His jacket was a casogue (*casóg*) and his hat was a caubeen (*cáibín*).

A lazy fellow was a scraiste (*scraiste*), an untidy housewife a streel (*straoil*). A fat man was a bodach (*bodach*); a teenage girl was a girsseagh (*girseach*). If she was hoarse she had a peechawn (*piocán*); a rash on her face was eyeraugh (*oighreach*). If she cried her mother hugged her and said 'What's wrong with you, a gra?' (*a grádh*), her grandfather called her mavourneen (*mo mhúirnín*), and the young lad who had his eye on her called her leannamachree (*leanbh mo chroí*). Her father said the boyfriend was only a glinkeen (*glincín*) and if he had his way he wouldn't let him within a scradasal (*scread asail*) of his little girl. Her older brother said the fellow was an amadawn (*amadán*). He was never any good at school and he used to smather (*smeadar*) his exercise book. If he was given a job to do he made a ballower (*baileabhair*) of it; he never knew how to keep his gob (*gob*) shut but clabbered (*clabar*) away like a lebidhe (*leibide*). He himself gave him a few palthogues (*poltóg*) one time but the fellow was strong, he caught him in a marafaisg (*marbh fáisc*) and belted him with his cithoge (*ciotóg*). It was meeaw (*mí-ádh*) to have tangled with him at all and he was lucky to get away. The next time they meet he'll have his camoge (*cámóg*) and he'll give him a leadoge (*leadóg*) or two with it that will leave him with a permanent lawang (*leath-mhaing*).

County Galway

Sheamusheen (*Séamuisín*) was a mean stucker (*stucaire*) who was a sheadeistach (*séid isteach*) or 'blow-in' to the townland. He never helped his neighbours, he didn't join the mehell (*meitheal*) at threshing time or when saving turf on the bog in summer.

He worked alone on the annagh (*annach*) and faslaugh (*fáslach*) where the sods of peat had been spread, making grogeens (*gróigín*) and doochawns (*duachán*) of them as they dried. He never wasted a single caorawn (*caorthán*) but gathered them up in a prashkeen (*praiscín*) and took them home to his wife for the fire. He was so busy working he had no time to watch the wild birds that inhabited the bog land: wheelawns (*faoileáin*), pelebeens (*pilibín*), crotachs (*crotach*), bunawn leines (*bunnán léine*) and long-legged cattyaddas (*ceataí fhada*). His back was sore from bending too long and he often got fairgorta (*féar gorta*) from hunger before evening. Shugawns (*siogán*), crawers (*crabhar*) and cuilogues (*cuileóg*) were the bane of his life when he sat on a tortoge (*tortóg*) to partake of the buttered coshgeen (*caisgín*) and cold tay (*té*) which his wife had packed for him in the cishawn (*ciseán*). If only there was a good shinawn (*síonnán*) of wind it would help to drive them away. At the end of the day his hands were full of gawgs (*gág*) and he had trawlach (*trálach*) in his wrists from lifting heavy sods. When he got home his wife gave him his dinner of cally (*cailli*) with milk, butter and two bugoges (*bog ubh*) laid by hens when the dog chased them from their nest box. His day wasn't finished yet. After dinner he threw a maum (*mám*) of oats to the garron (*gearrán*) and a sop (*sop*) of hay to the calves and set off to look after the sheep. One of them had a spohawn (*spothán*) under her jowl and had to be dosed against fluke. Another that suffered from galarnagat (*galar na gcat*) was blind. The rest of the flock had left their pasture because the stonewalls were breached. Whoever built them didn't construct a proper fideen (*fidín*) at the base with spalls (*spál*) and didn't put in a pooreen (*púirthín*) to allow the sheep free passage from one field to the next. Because of the broken fences he had to put a booreen (*búithrín*) on the ass and a cromnask (*cromhnasc*) on a thieving cow to prevent the animals from trespassing on his neighbour. If they strayed there'd be rooleybooley (*ruaille buaille*) when the neighbour found out.

Sheamusheen and his wife lived in a thatched bohawn (*bothán*) with a bunthop (*bun sop*) coming down over the window. They had only one child, a putach (*putach*) of six years who was a mashteen (*maistín*) and demanded a lot of attention. He hadn't massmadra (*meas madra*) on his father who tried to please him, and in his tantrums he often made smithereens (*smidirín*) of a mug or plate given him with his food. His mother took him with her when she went for the cows and showed him traneens (*tráithnín*), boohalawn (*buachalán*), noneens (*nóinín*) and glorawns (*glórán*), thinking that he might be a naturalist when he grew up. But all the lad did was to throw scraws (*scraith*) at her and put crawdawns (*crádán*) in her hair. Losing patience with him on one occasion she gave him a ladoge (*leadóg*) on the bottom with the palm of her hand. At that he ran away from her and got stuck in a scrawglugar (*scraith ghlugar*) where he almost drowned. Afterward she tried to plawmaus (*plámás*) him and promised him sweets if he was good, all to no avail – he was very stoocach (*stuacach*).

Ceilidheing (*céilidhe*) was a favourite pastime in rural areas during long winter nights. Men gathered every night in a rambling house to swap stories by the fireside or to play cards. A game often went on until the small hours resulting in players walking home in darkness. Having listened to stories about sheeogues (*síóg*), banshees (*bean sidhe*) and the coishte mara (*cóiste marbh*), anybody who gave heed to pishrogues (*pisreóg*) was liable to be frightened by a farbrega (*fear bréige*) erected at a crossroads or a wailing cry from behind the bushes. This was regarded as fun but sometimes a person was genuinely put on the shachrawn (*seachrán*) by the fodeen mara (*fóidín meartha*), a will-of-the-wisp light that led him around in a confused state or left him sitting on his gogadhe (*gogaide*) in the middle of a field not knowing which way to turn for home. One man who was on the dulamugh (*dul amú*) reckoned that he saw the pooka (*púca*), the most dreaded of all apparitions, on his way home from a card game one night. He thought at first that it was a human giant until he got a look at the croobs (*crúb*). He knew then that it was the devil himself. His mates suggested that he had been drinking too much poteen (*poitín*), that what he saw was a big jackass, but he firmly believed that it was the 'auld' boy. He gave up playing cards and stayed home at night afterwards, much to the delight of his wife and family. She herself had clayheen (*cléithín*), a condition that caused her great pain in her chest and their twelve-year-old had a bunool (*bunamhail*) from going barefoot. He hurt his lyraceen (*laidhraicín*) too when he climbed to a magpie's nest in an effort to catch the scaltawns (*scaltán*) before they started to fly. He tried to lift a granoge (*gráinneóg*) once but his hands were pricked all over from the needles. He had better success with the droleen (*dreoilín*) that he caught on St Stephen's Day. Putting it into a tinsel covered box he and his pal went round with the 'wran' and got money and sweet cake from their more generous neighbours. Others said they were a pair of corrachawns (*corrachán*) and they gave them bata agus bohar (*bata agus bóthar*).

At school the master taught the pupils about nature and wildlife which he asked them to respect, and never to throw stones at birds or raid their nests. He told them that God gave us wild birds and animals for our use and benefit, not for destruction. On a fine summer day he took them out to a field near the school, where he pointed out various wild plants: rannach (*rainneach*), brawste (*bráiste*), shelistrum (*seillistrim*), feoran (*feorán*), rideoge (*rideóg*). He didn't have to identify the nantoge (*neantóg*); nettles had stung them all on many occasions. On a turlough (*turloch*) he showed them deposits of white marl (*márla bán*) left behind by retreating floods over thousands of years and pointed out the soomera (*súmaire*) through which flooding disappeared when water levels became low in nearby rivers and lakes. He told them they should look for different species of plants such as cannawaun (*ceannabhán*) and seisk (*seisc*) in the bog and farnoge (*fearnóg*) and sally (*sailleóg*) bushes on wet land and in this way become familiar with all aspects of nature.

The aforementioned are but a cross-section of anglicised Irish words commonly used in everyday language during my childhood. It would be impossible at this stage to recall them in their entirety. A variety of expressions used in describing individuals tended to be deprecatory – bostune (*bostún*), scraiste (*scraiste*), ceolawne (*ceolán*), spriosawn (*spriosán)*, gedameen (*geidimín*), edawl (*éadál*), loodramawn (*lúdramán*), gobarloo (*gob ar liú*), strap (*straip*), stucker (*stuacaire*), anishore (*annaiseór*), are a few that spring to mind. Other terms related to farm and household articles: ruoge (*ruadhóg*), waxed thread for stitching shoes and harness; durneen (*doirnín*) a handgrip on the shaft of a scythe; poreen (*póirthín*), a small potato; bocklogue (*bachlóg*), a sprout; cosawn (*casán*), a path; gansey (*geansaí*), a jumper; keenagh (*caonach*), moss – the list is endless. '*A mhic, a stór, a chuid*' were terms of endearment while '*G'mach as seo*' (Be off out of here) and '*Siúil leat*' (be on your way) indicated the opposite. At this point it might be appropriate for the writer to desist also.
"*Slán agus Beannacht.*"

COUNTY KERRY

Mary O'Connor recalls episodes from life in her native Lixnaw, County Kerry, in the thirties and forties.

CHRISTMAS AND TURKEYS

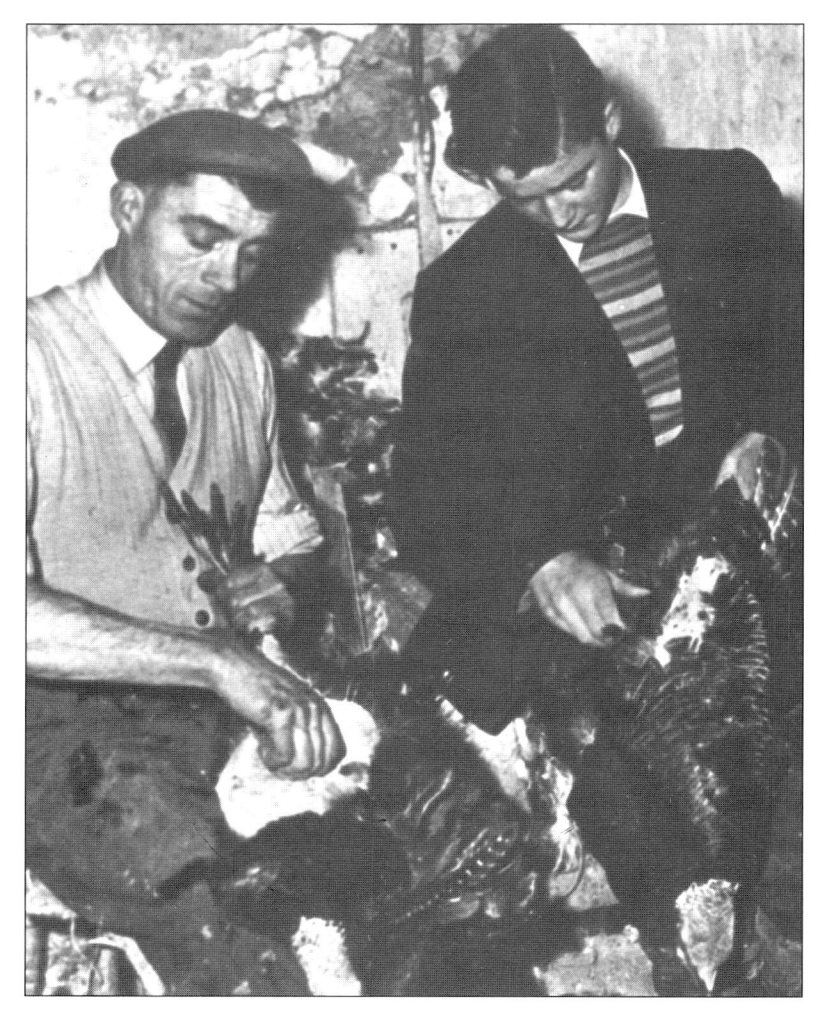

Plucking Turkeys

Every year my mother would set a few clutches of turkey eggs in about late spring. They took four weeks to hatch. Great care was taken of them in that time. When they were due to come out my mother would hold the eggs up towards the light. If there was a space at the top they were safe enough; if she shook eggs that were doubtful and they made a rattling sound they were called *gluggers* (non-productive) and were thrown out. When the young turkeys were hatched out they had to be kept warm. We had to cut up nettles and other greens very fine for their feed. My mother often fed them scrambled eggs. When they were older they were fed on meal. When Christmas came they were brought to the market and sold. My mother was very proud of her turkey money. We all got something nice for Christmas.

My father reared a couple of pigs. He fed them by boiling *poreens* (small potatoes) for them and mixing in meal and skimmed milk. Pigs are not dirty as some people think. They never soil their own beds. They roll in muck in the hot weather to protect their skin from the sun. When my father killed a pig he would send fresh meat, called *drisheens*, around to the neighbours. The black pudding was also shared with them. The neighbours in their turn did the same.

My brother made a football out of the pig's bladder. Sometimes my father kept a sow and she would have a litter of bonhams. We often had to sit up with them at night when they were little. There was always a weakling in the litter that was called a runt. The mother sow was very vicious. We had a dividing rail between us and the pigs, as she was very protective of her young. I always felt very sad when the pigs were taken away and sold at the market.

SUMMER TIME

Going back about fifty years we had lovely summers. The men were out in the bog in the month of May. We had long days of sunshine when we took off our shoes and stretched our toes in the brown boggy soil as we footed and clamped the turf. We brought out a billycan of water and someone would light a fire and boil the water. We would eat big wedges of soda bread. Sometimes they would boil a smaller can of water and drop in a few fresh eggs, have a good feast and then start back into the work again. Then there was the cutting and raking of the hay. I loved getting spins on the long hay cart when they brought home the hay. We seemed to have great long spells of sunshine.

The Forge

There was the threshing of the corn, with the humming and the droning of the machine, and so many neighbours coming to help out. A man or two on the machine fed in the sheaves of corn and two more men filled the bags with grain at the back of the machine. Brown earthenware jars of porter were passed around to the men. I remember a simple, innocent man who always followed the threshing machine. In fact he was called 'Thrash'. I never knew what his real name was or where he came from. He always carried a hurley with him and had a big watch with a long chain hanging from his waistcoat pocket. He never could tell the time and people would ask him, 'What is the time?' He always said, 'Ten to two', and so ten to two was always called Thrash's time. He was found drowned in a bog hole some years later. He was fond of the 'hard stuff'.

We used to have a travelling man coming to our house. If the weather was very bad my father made up a bed of straw in the kitchen for him and kept a big fire lighting. He could never turn him away. Bob Landers was his name. He had a very long grey beard – he would have made a great Santa Claus. I often wonder what would happen if the youth of today were transported back in time to see the hard working conditions of that era – no electricity, no proper sanitation and no washing machines. I think they would go into deep shock. But in those days we had a lot of sunshine and we were happy.

Another nice memory I have is of the blacksmith's forge where we would get a turn at the bellows. The blacksmith was a big jolly man. I loved to watch him lifting the shoes out of the very hot fire, hammering them into shape, fitting them to the horse's hoof and then immersing them in cold water. I loved the smell of the forge. I still remember it after so many years.

OUR FEATHERED FRIENDS

My mother always had hens, turkeys and ducks. I loved to eat a lovely blue duck egg for breakfast. I ran out one morning to the hen house to get some eggs. I was a giddy young one. I scaled a reek of hay on my way and slid down the other side. Some careless person had left a pitchfork flat on the ground, and one of the prongs went up through my foot. My father had to pull it out while my brother held me. There was no trip to casualty or a doctor. My father just poured clean paraffin oil in the wound and that was the end of that.

Going back to the hens, we had mixed breeds – Anconas, White Leghorns and Rhode Island Reds. They used to say, 'A whistling woman or a crowing hen would put the devil out of his den'. Well, we had such a hen. She would try crowing in a kind of hoarse voice; she even tried mating with the other hens. She never laid eggs so she was non-productive. My mother always killed a rooster for St Martin's night on November 11. She would put the blood on to a white cloth, wrap it up, and put it under the roof beams for a year. So that was how the queer old (lesbian / hermaphrodite) hen finished up. I really don't know what was the origin of the ritual. Was St Martin a martyr or a soldier?

My mother always kept turkeys. She would bring the female turkey to our neighbour, Mag's, turkey cock. She would ask me to come along with her as my mother complained of a bad back. I was mortified. The male turkey would do a dance round the turkey for a while, and my neighbour's son would look at me in a coy way. I was learning about the birds and the bees and so I took up the signals. People in the country were always so much in touch with nature and people from the city were really the *'gombeens'*. We knew where calves came from and we knew where lambs came from, so we had an inkling where babies came from. We didn't really believe that the midwife brought the baby in her black bag but I wasn't too sure about that.

We had a lovely golden thatched roof on our house. My father took great pride in his thatching. He would have us paring the 'scallops' as he called them. I think it was to peg in the thatch. He would take great care with his work. He harvested acre upon acre of wheat and made *sugán* chairs out of the wheaten straw. He would have my mother twisting the *sugáns* with him. She wound the straw round a small stick and as he fed more straw into the rope she had to keep moving and twisting the straw. They were so happy together. They would sit by the big turf fire at night, just like young lovers, even though they had six of us. They would reminisce about their house dances and, 'Do you remember this?' and 'Do you remember that?' My mother had to go to hospital once – she had a hernia – and my father cried like a child. He thought that she was dying. When she was coming home he had us shining and polishing every place. We were all so happy when she came home. We didn't have much money but we had wealth in our love for one another.

COUNTY LEITRIM

Bridget Gunnigle has vivid memories of life in Kinlough, North Leitrim, when she was young.

MAY 1929
PREPARING FOR FIRST COMMUNION IN
EDENVILLE NATIONAL SCHOOL, KINLOUGH

Holy Communion Outfits

Set off for school 8.50 am, sunny May morning
Cotton dresses, shoeless feet, clutching catechism.
Up the steps, two more weeks to go
First Communion children in front seats
Morning prayers, Miss McGloin.
'Everyone learn their questions last night?' 'Yes, Miss'
'Say an Act of Contrition', chorus of voices,
From 9am to 10am for a whole month.
Fear, tears, slaps, arms, legs, hands, anywhere, didn't matter.
To the chapel on Fridays from 6.30 to 7.30pm.
Fr Grey, big man, hair pulled, ears pulled, boxed on the head,

County Leitrim

Twenty-three of us, thirteen girls and ten boys
Shouts, threats, mortal sins, burning in hell.
'What's a mortal sin? – 'Missing Mass,
Disobeying your parents, stealing, telling lies'.
O Lord, don't want to go to hell, devils all round me.
Time up, run from the chapel yard, heads full of catechism,
Will it last till school on Monday?
Supper, bed, can't sleep, out to the chamber pot,
Back in bed, out again,
Mary, my sister. 'Shut up and go to sleep. You have me annoyed'.
Nightmares, horns on my forehead,
Mother shaking the holy water.
At long last the final Friday, finished with Fr Grey.
Rushed from the chapel laughing, crying, at the same time,
Down to Ellie Cormac Dan's shop, pennyworth of caramels,
Halfpenny worth of Cleeve's toffee, Peggy's leg, liquorice pipes.
Rose Moore lost her penny; we all shared with her.
Laughing, licking, chewing, over the back way to Bosco's.
Black can on the coals, making tea, duck egg boiling
In the black porringer. 'Play a tune on the flute, Bosco'.
'Get out, bad scram to the lot of ye. Fr Grey will put horns on ye'
'We're finished with him, we got our tickets', we shouted.
Pause on the footpath, get our hoops. No, get our skipping ropes.
Up and down the footpath, Jim Joe's ass and cart at Denis's shop
Putting on meal and flour. Jim Deegan the tinker coming
Drunk out of Jimmy's, the two children sitting on the spring cart,
Nora Mangan feeding them hot milk, bread, the mother begging
Round the town somewhere. Play marbles on the corner.
Big boys won't let us, getting late, all go home.
Saturday, wash in the tin bath, carbolic soap.
Sunday the big day, up at six o'clock, Mass at eleven.
Sister's white dress with flounces at the bottom

Hearths and Homesteads

Long sleeves, long white stockings, white crochet gloves,
No flesh allowed to be seen, no curlers, no short fringe,
Would have liked ringlets. 'Hair too fine,' mother said.
Rose Moore had lovely ones, her mother made them with rags.
Got confession on the Saturday, big box, fearful.
Please God don't let me forget the Act of Contrition.
In the front seats in the chapel, boys on one side,
Girls on the other. Uragh and Buckode schools as well.
White veil held in place with ribbon and hair slides
Meeting pals at the chapel gate, admiring each other's dresses.
In to Mass, Fr Dineen on the altar,
Miss McGloin holding our heads makes sure we don't bite
The Communion, another mortal sin, swallow it whole.
Out from Mass, mothers chatting, fathers chatting,
Everyone in new clothes, 'How much did you get?'

'How much did you get?' whispers, pennies rattling in bags,
Grannies two shillings, aunts, uncles one shilling,
Tommy Murray sixpence, John Clancy, threepenny bit,
More neighbours, pennies, bag getting heavier.
Mary Horan has half-crowns but her father is a doctor,
Her dress was lovely too, white silk with little blue birds
Embroidered on it. It was a shop dress; ours made by mothers.
Eileen Brennan's hair was lovely, all ringlets,
Rose McMorrow's was the same.
Paddy Morley's hackney car brought us all to Bundoran.
What to buy? A swimsuit was two shillings, bathing cap tenpence,
A penny to share bathing box.
Dinner in Igoe's eating house, Mr Igoe gave me threepence.
My bag full of money, mother and father said, 'Spend away at it
But buy something for my sister and brothers'.
Bundoran rock, a penny ice cream, wafers a penny,

Hobby horses twopence, swing boats, dodgems,
Fortunetellers, black man eating fire,
Us all goggle-eyed.
Six o'clock home - what a day!

GRANNY

Last week we had a power cut that lasted a few hours and my first reaction was to complain about the sheer inconvenience of it all. Later on as I sat in the flickering light of a candle its peaceful glow helped me to see things more clearly and I began to reflect on how we take electricity for granted. We hardly ever think of how easy it is to have instant light, to have heat at hand for cooking, to watch TV or to relax with a good book. And I breathed a prayer for whatever person or persons made this invention possible, and then I remembered . . .

In the candlelight by the window my granny loved to sit
Watching the evening shadows fall. Sometimes she would knit.
Then she would take the candle up the stairs to bed
And leave it on the dresser, as her prayers she said.
We children gathered round her and held her ageing hand.
She told us little stories of fairies and fairyland,
Of crocks of gold, rainbows, and leprechauns dressed in green,
And pookas dropping turnips down the chimney at Halloween.
She was our friend and confidant, we told her of our woes.
She helped with our spellings and kissed better our bruised toes.
And when we went to bed at night she'd wait till we were asleep,
Then she'd shake the holy water and blow the candle out.
Now Granny has long since departed to the land of roses fair,
Her chair is by the window, but there's no candle lighting there.

COUNTY SLIGO

Nora Oates writes of rural life in Grange, Co Sligo, in her youth.

LIVING CONDITIONS MANY YEARS AGO

When I was growing up in the country every house burned turf. All had a hearth fire with a crook over it on which to hang the oven or pot or kettle. We reckoned that in any house that had a grate the people must be well off and lucky as well. Some turf had red ashes and every woman hated the red ash turf. Maybe it was the colour that made it more obvious, but the red ash seemed to go everywhere. Nobody we knew had a range or burned coal, except the O'Malleys who owned the local pub and grocery shop. We thought they must be very well off.

At that time most countrywomen wore a 'pinny' or black apron and a lot of the older women took snuff. They kept it in one of those small oval-shaped tins and they were very secretive about it because the men didn't like them to use it. The little tins started life full of Coleman's dry mustard and came in very useful for the bit of snuff. Most of the older women also had their hair long and it was put up in a bun, or plaited and wound round their heads. The women never went anywhere except to Mass or to the Stations (where people took it in turn to have Mass said in the house) or to the local shop. There was no supermarket then or no girls' night out! Sometimes there'd be a parcel from America and maybe some money too. The clothes from America were lovely, from another world, and the women would be swanking in them and wearing them to Mass; women seldom went to town.

Of course there was no electricity then; rural electrification was away in the future. The oil lamp provided the light, and in the winter, we used to put a hairpin on the globe in case the frost would crack it. If the globe was broken we had to fall back on candlelight until someone going to town could get another one.

Children went barefoot to school in the summer; in the winter they wore shoes or boots. There was no school transport; everyone had to walk. Breakfast was porridge or an egg if the hens were laying. There was no convenience food and no 'fifty-seven varieties' of cereals. A lot of families killed a pig for meat for the winter. We brought our lunch to school, usually soda bread and a bottle of milk. If we did get shop bread, or loaf bread as we called it, it was a treat. There was no central heating, only a small turf fire in the schoolroom and very often the teacher stood with his or her back to it.

In the autumn we had to pick blackberries for jam. We didn't mind that so much as we liked jam. Blackberry and apple was nice and also vegetable marrow and, I think, ginger. We loved jam when we were young and now I hardly ever eat it. I wonder do kids eat it now or are their tastes more sophisticated? There was no running water then. Young ones got the job of going for water for the house and filling the tubs for cattle. There was no sanitation either but that is too painful to talk about, especially the nettles. How did we ever manage to grow up? We never locked our doors and if you went to a neighbour's house you never knocked on the door or they would think you were strange.

MAKING THE HAY

The generation before us took haymaking very seriously. In that era men cut hay with scythes. They'd start cutting very early in the morning and stop before the real heat of the day. They used to have little three-quart cans of water, as it was very thirsty work.

They'd leave the cans in the shade and drink as they required it. The little cans used to come into the shops with sweets and nearly every house had a few of them.

The hay was left for a day or two and then shaken out to dry. Everyone gave a hand; children had to help too. Men used pitchforks for this and it was a tedious job. If there was any danger of rain the hay was lapped, that is made into little bundles. You had to roll each bit of hay into a bundle making sure that the air could get through it to dry it. If the weather was fine and dry the hay was usually built into cocks, or sometimes built into hand shakings or rucks. These weren't very big and were easy to make. There was a horse-drawn gadget called a tumbling paddy to gather in the hay.

There was a knack to building hay into tramp cocks. There were always one or two men in the neighbourhood who were good at it. They were greatly sought after and there was a bit of rivalry between them. The neighbours pitched in and helped each other and everyone was glad to see the hay off the ground. Then it was brought to the haggard or small garden near the house to be made into a rick. There was a horse-drawn machine called a float that had a long, flat, wooden base and an iron lever with steel ropes attached to each side. The ropes were put round the haycock and the lever hauled it on to the float with a winch. An ass or a pony brought in the hand shakings. Ropes which went round the hay were attached to the harness and they were pulled into the haggard in that way.

There was no tractor or heavy machinery then. I still remember the lovely clean smell of hay. Very often when the hay was saved there would be a 'hooley'. Silage was not even thought of or heard of then.

CUTTING THE TURF

There was a time when every country house in Ireland had a stack of turf to see them through the winter and town dwellers used the turf as well. Days on the bog were so hard. In April men usually started cutting the turf. If the weather was wet they'd have to wait until May. Men often had to travel long distances to the bog. A few men would go together and work together. They would bring their lunch, usually soda bread, milk for the tea and a few eggs. When they decided to eat they'd make a fire and boil the water for the tea. Often the tea and sugar were thrown into the kettle when it boiled – I suppose that's how bad tea used to be called 'bog water'. The eggs would be boiled in an old 'ponny' or tin mug.

Turf Stacked and Saved

They'd start work by cleaning the turf bank that is, digging the sods off the top of it. Sometimes the sods were tough – they were called 'scraws' or 'kebee' – full of roots, probably heather, making it hard work. When the bank was clean the men started cutting the turf sods with turf spades. There was a right-hand spade and a left-hand one for anyone who was a 'citeog'. They'd cut the turf about 8 to 10 inches deep, that being the depth of the spit, and when that section was done they'd start another spit. The man cutting threw the sods up to a man on the bank who would have to wheel them out with a turf barrow, heel them out to dry and spread them.

Weather permitting they were left to dry for a week or so. When dry they were footed, that is six or seven sods were put standing on their ends, with one on top to prevent the rain going down through them. Then they'd be clamped or put into little stacks ready to be brought home, always of course, depending on the weather. Nowadays there are machines to cut the turf: it's very labour saving, the sods look like sausages. I don't think there are many people using turf now; everyone seems to have oil or electric heating. The turf was brought home by ass cart or horse cart. Then men started to buy lorries and they were welcome because they could bring home a good load. If the weather was good I think the men enjoyed a day on the bog. They'd exchange news and discuss the crops and the price of cattle. But time brings changes – all that is changed now. Many aspects of country life are changed, maybe it's for the best. I don't know.

SLIGO TOWN

Bernie Gilbride gives a vivid picture of a bygone Sligo Town, so different in its buildings and the way of life there now.

THE MARKET YARD, SLIGO

As I parked my car in the Market Yard the other morning I got to thinking of all the changes there over the past few years, and wondered what the old neighbours in Temple Street would make of it all if they could come back and see it now. The entire centre has been cleared away. The three massive gates are gone and it is open to drive or walk through at any hour.

My earliest recollection of the yard is of a huge fire on the left-hand side as one enters from Temple Street. I was being held up to an attic window so that I could see the flames. I have since discovered it had been a shirt factory and its burning down was catastrophic for our small town at that time. Being very young this aspect of the fire meant nothing to me, but the flames really took my fancy, much as fireworks do for children today.

At that time the yard was completely enclosed, having three massive gates: one at each entrance, to Temple St., to High St. and to Dominic St. These gates were 15 to 20 feet high and so heavy. They were padlocked each evening at 6pm and re-opened each morning at 7am. A caretaker who lived in a house in the yard did this. I can still see the huge keys that hung from his belt. Inside the gates were stores on either side of the yard. I would assume that these stores were once dwelling houses, but at that time they held all sorts of equipment for Sligo Corporation. Just inside the Temple St. gate was a big watering trough, continuously overflowing, for the horses to drink from.

The entire centre of the yard was covered and slated, with a large open-ended platform at either end. In between was an open space

Sligo Town

capable of taking at least 10 to 12 horses and carts. The platforms, I thought, were of solid stone covered in very heavy timber similar to railway sleepers and were the height of the normal cart, so that the cart drawn alongside was easily unloaded. On each platform were huge scales capable of weighing anything and everything. On these same platforms we youngsters sang and danced if we had a chance, practising for when we would all be famous film stars. To be in the 'pictures' was everyone's ambition then. Alas, I don't think any of us realised that dream.

Every Saturday morning would see the yard full of horses, carts and farmers with all their wares: hay, potatoes, cabbage plants (when in season), oats, turf and blocks. There were so many carts they overflowed into Temple St. lining both sides. One could see the bargaining going on: the farmers with their big cocks of hay overhanging the carts showing the good quality, the buyer sticking his hand into the centre of the hay, pulling out a handful, smelling it, running it through his fingers. Then the bargaining would begin, with much walking away and arguing the price until eventually a deal was made, with a spit on the hand and a handshake. The money was handed over, and the 'luck' money handed back. Often there were carts of bonhams and their squeals could be heard way down in O'Connell St. Carts in which young calves with their velvety, soft, frightened eyes occasionally allowed their noses to be rubbed.

In fact on Saturday morning, Market Day, the place was a seething mass of humanity, with animals, produce, horses and carts for good measure. And the noise – much shouting, laughter, neighing of horses, braying of donkeys, squealing of bonhams and the odd fiddle or melodeon being played and of course, dogs barking – a lively place indeed. On Temple St. corner stood a pub. It too would be filled with farmers and buyers all during the market and many a deal was sealed with a drink, with much of the 'luck' money being spent on drink. Another pub stood at the High St. entrance. All along High St. were many shops that complemented the country trade, selling grain, groceries and huge blocks of salt. The hardware stores sold spades, forks, rakes and all sorts of farming implements.

This was not the only use for the yard. Sligo Corporation used it to store its equipment for making and repairing roads - sand, gravel, stones, a big stone crusher, a huge steamroller, barrels and barrels of tar, a tar spreader which had a fire underneath to keep the tar bubbling and spreadable and the smell from that permeated the whole area. There was a water sprinkler to wash down the streets after the market. The town fire tenders lived there too and the firemen lived in the neighbouring area as there were very few cars and no mobile phones. In fact one of the first phones was installed in the fire tender sheds. Outside the gates was an emergency bell behind glass, to be broken if the place was locked in order to raise the alarm. Then the gate nearest the fire was opened and off they went. The town brass band had a place there too and could be heard, and sometimes seen, practising on Sunday mornings or summer evenings, much to our delight. During the war the Local Defence Force used the yard for drilling and marching and this we loved to see.

Now as I sit here all around me are modern elegant apartments with beautiful balconies. Where once the old stores stood, once again are dwelling places. The yard is completely open with through roads to Temple St., High St. and Dominic St. and lots and lots of car parking spaces. It's only five minutes walk from the town centre and so is a very popular spot for parking. Having parked I must be going, and must not forget to put up my ticket, otherwise it may cost me 20 euro instead of 65 cent for the ticket.

No doubt the old neighbours would have much to amaze them: a woman parking a car, the number of cars around, having to pay to leave the car for even an hour, but most of all, the now completely open yard.

GAMES FROM LONG AGO

In these dark wintry evenings my mind wanders back to blazing coal fires and lots of books for reading. My youth came long before television, in fact before even radio became commonplace, so we had to make our own entertainment. Spring, summer, autumn, winter, each season had its own games but winter was my favourite, as I loved to read.

Spring was our skipping season, too chilly to stand about, but with heavy winter gear shed, skipping was just the thing. We had special skipping ropes with painted wooden handles, shaped for hands to get a firm grip. We started with ten straight skips. To do this without tripping at the start of the season would be most satisfactory, when three or four of us were keeping time with each other. As we became more adept we would cross the rope over our heads and under foot in time to the count. When a group gathered many hours were spent by most of us running in and out between the twists of a long heavy rope, being wound by two members on turn, no nice handles this time. When disaster struck and one tripped, the winders were invariably accused of winding too fast or faltering. It was never one's own clumsiness, and many a row ensued.

Hearths and Homesteads

In summer we played shop in back yards or gardens, or hopscotch on the pavements. Shop was everyone's favourite and could last a whole day. All empty jars, boxes and packets were carefully saved over winter for these shops. Our tea consisted of dock seeds, the flat leaves were slices of bread, sea sand was the sugar and clay mixed with water were mudcakes when dry. Our shop was a long plank on two big stones and the money was 'channies' – pieces of broken delph – readily available in most back yards or shrubbery. As one usually had the onerous task of minding a smaller sibling, great care had to be taken as they were quite capable of sampling some of the wares, causing much trouble and washing out of mouths, all afraid of parental wrath.

Hopscotch was very popular too. Beds were marked out on the flagstone pavements, numbered one to six, with number six being a broad flag so one could rest both feet before the hazardous trip back to number one, often having to hop over a flag owned by one of the players. We threw a marker onto a flag, hopped along on one leg, picked it up and hopped back. But if one slipped or missed the correct flag with the marker, one had to begin again and so the game went on and on. This being summer we were in our bare feet, and how we loved to feel the heat from the warm flagstones on our feet, so good for our eyesight or so we were told.

'Statues' was another group game. The leader stood facing the wall and counted to ten, while the others ran as near to him as they dared. When he turned round, if you were caught moving so much as a finger, you were out. Steps, was again controlled by the leader. All sorts of steps were allotted: baby steps, scissors, trains and giant steps, all enabling one to try and overtake the leader. The first to reach him was the next leader. Tip cat was played with two sticks and much guessing. Marbles or taws were usually played along the gutters, much to the annoyance of parents.

Autumn was conker time. Strong conkers were gathered in the woods, carefully dried, bored and threaded onto pieces of strong string with a secure double knot under the conker. These were tested against each other and the one that succeeded in breaking others was a valuable commodity, which could be traded for comics or books, which brings me back to my favourite.

Winter evenings were for reading, though we also had board games such as Ludo, Lotto and Snakes and Ladders. If we were lucky and had snow or heavy frost, then we went sliding or tobogganing on the hilly fields around the town if we were allowed. There was many a tumble and often a sore arm or leg, bravely borne with no complaint, just in case one was not allowed out to join in the fun again.

Once the snow and frost disappeared and the evenings began to stretch it was skipping time again, and I will leave you with a sample of the rhymes we sang, while playing hopscotch and skipping.
Tinker, tailor. soldier, sailor, rich man, poor man, beggarman, thief, (one married into whichever trade one missed a skip on).
London Bridge is falling down, falling down, falling down,
London Bridge is falling down, my fair lady.
What did the robbers do to you, do to you, do to you?
What did the robbers do to you, my fair lady?
And, of course,
Ring a ring a rosie, a pocket full of posies,
Attishoo, Attishoo, we all fall down. (This rhyme is a souvenir of the dreaded plague.)
Jump, Jump over the moon.
If you never come back, it will be too soon.

A TOWNIE'S DAY ON THE BOG

I had never been to the bog, and on hearing my husband say that he was going, begged to be brought, as I knew nothing much about turf. Now our bog was on a shelf to the north of Benbulbin and sat in a horse shoe of mountains, its front looking out over Grange and Streedagh, with Sligo bay to the left and the Donegal mountains and bay to the north. Classiebawn Castle and even Inishmurray Island were almost at our feet, because of the height of the shelf, giving us fantastic views all around. The silence was what struck me first; just the chirp of insects, the odd bleat of a lamb and the gurgling sounds of the mountain streams as they tumbled down the mountain over rocky beds on their way to the sea.

The turf bank was warm with a hard crust, but springy and soft underneath. The cutting had been done some weeks earlier, and it was now time to make 'footings' so that the turf would dry and harden for saving. A footing consists of five or six wet turf sods, built to stand on their ends, leaning towards each other, forming a triangle, with one sod sitting on top. Backbreaking work, all that stooping, but I had been warned, even discouraged from going. So I didn't dare complain and just got on with it.

There were many families similarly engaged, and many called to chat thus giving us a break. Of course the fire was lit and tea was made on a regular basis, any excuse was good enough! Tea on the bog is like no other tea you have ever tasted. The kettle being boiled on the open fire gives it a slightly smoky flavour, and then it was always so strong – as the saying goes, you could trot a mouse on it. The bottle of milk was kept cool in a bog hole; fresh homemade bread with country butter, tasted like manna from heaven after working outdoors. After dinner it was our time to go visiting and I met many neighbours I had only heard of before. Many of the men there only met on the bog or on fair days, so much news had to be exchanged.

Working at the Turf Face

By evening our turf bank was covered with hundreds of footings all black and shiny. As we went home all the talk was of the weather and what might be expected. It was imperative that the footings dried soon, so that clamps might be made. Because of the position of the bog, being overhung by Benbulbin, only a few weeks were available when the sun was at its highest to dry and season the turf.

Coming back down the old mountain road with the sun now beginning to sink, casting its golden glow over land and sea, I wished time could stand still and let me savour the beauty of the view, the magic of that quietness and peace for just a little longer.

But it was time to go and all too soon we were back in so-called civilisation – cars, bustle and noise. That year the turf dried to hard black sods, and when they were brought home they were built into a stack that kept us warm all winter. Mountain turf dries almost as hard as coal, and I loved its cheery blaze.

I never again worked on the bog. Shortly afterwards oil became the fashion and we had central heating installed. For years I lit no fire, but now with more time on my hands, I often have an open fire again. I still delight in the smell and appearance of a good turf fire recalling with pleasure the day I made footings on Lyle bog in the shadow of Benbulbin.

TOBERNALT

From my youngest days Tobernalt, or the Holy Well as it is sometimes called, has held a special fascination for me. It is there that I go to give thanks for the many blessings I enjoy, or with requests for special needs. Often I go just to absorb its peace and tranquillity, in stark contrast to the hectic schedule of modern living. So where or what is Tobernalt?

Tobernalt is an ancient, pagan assembly place, approximately three miles east of Sligo town, near the shores of Lough Gill. In pagan times it is reputed to have been the place of festivities to celebrate the old god *Lúgh,* who gave the Irish name *Lughnasa* to the month of August. Its religious connotations go back to the mists of Celtic times, and when Christianity came to Ireland, this religious aspect simply became part of the Christian ethos down through the centuries. Perhaps this is why Garland Sunday, the last Sunday in July, has special associations with Tobernalt.

As the word *tobar* meaning a well indicates there is a spring well here from which clear, icy water continuously flows in a stream to Lough Gill. For as long as I can remember there is a beautiful altar, cut from the rocky face of a heavily wooded hill, which shelters this place and gives it its air of seclusion and mystery. The Sisters of Mercy in Sligo built this particular altar, in thanksgiving for the saving of the inhabitants of Sligo from a virulent fever long before my day. Perhaps it replaced an older altar, as we are assured it had been used for sacrificial rites for centuries.

Holy Well and Mass Rock

As one approaches the copse of trees at the entrance to Tobernalt, one usually stands still by a large rock to look around in the shady dim light. Tradition says that St. Patrick rested here on his way from Lough Derg and left the imprint of his hand on the rock. To this day one can stretch one's fingers and thumb to fit the indentations on its smooth surface.

On looking upwards to the altar one is taken with its rugged beauty and feels at once that this a holy, hidden place. The well immediately before you is gurgling its water to a little stream, falling gently over its rocky bed to the lake a couple of hundred yards away. The well itself is surrounded by a thick stone wall approximately three foot high, with an entrance down three or four stone-cut steps, much worn by the many feet down the years. In this wall is a niche, specifically incorporated to hold a 'porringer' with which to drink the water. The water is icy cold and so refreshing coming as it does from the solid rock. It is reported to have medicinal qualities and generations have drunk there hoping to be cured of their many ailments. It is especially recommended for eye ailments of all sorts. Some people have left bits of rags and walking sticks hanging on the trees, as proof of their belief and devotion. The devotion I heard of as a child was that of the 'nine Tuesdays' which was no mean feat at that time as the road was a stony rough track with not much transport available. We loved this water. Having walked the three miles from town, it was very welcome and refreshing, and the perfect accompaniment to our simple picnics, usually bread and jam with an apple if we were lucky. We never minded the long walk as we came with friends. Knowing every twist and turn of the road the miles simply fell away. We viewed the lake from the hilltops – our lake – enjoyed the smell of the woods and the damp shrubbery, even the smell of the wild garlic growing so profusely under the trees. On arrival, having eaten and rested, we proceeded to say our prayers. Leaving the wild flowers we had gathered on the way at Our Lady's feet, we made the Stations of the Cross. This we enjoyed as we went from one stone to another, each marked with a roman numeral, and scattered in between the trees, on either side of the stream, so that we had to go over and back on the wooden planks, much to our delight. The actual prayers said, I am sure, were easily counted.

Tobernalt was especially useful during Penal times from 1691, after the defeat of King James at the Battle of the Boyne, to Catholic Emancipation in 1829, enacted under the persuasion and guidance of Daniel O'Connell. All during those years the celebration of Mass was prohibited, and every priest had a price on his head. Because of its location, Tobernalt was an ideal spot for flouting this law, and with lookouts at the top of the hill and along the shore, priests were relatively safe there. So it has continued down the years to be a place of pilgrimage and celebration.

The main celebration at Tobernalt was, of course, held on Garland Sunday. How we prayed it would be fine and never minded rising in the early hours at about 5am to make first mass at 7am. The road would be crowded with whole families of people on foot like ourselves. Everyone knew everyone else, so there was much chatting and laughter, which shortened the journey. Some older people said the rosary. These we avoided like the plague. Those who had boats came by river and lake, much to our envy, while some came by pony and trap. On a sunny morning it was a delight to walk in the freshness of early day, sometimes to see the mist vanish as the sun came up over the lake. During the Mass everyone joined in the hymn singing with the choir. Hymn singing in the open air is different. It's as if it goes straight to God in His Heavenly Kingdom. There were no radios in those days and a good singer was much appreciated. If singing came from a boat on the lake, it could be heard and enjoyed all around the shore, water being a great carrier of sound.

On the green nearby there were many stalls, selling all sorts of religious objects: rosary beads, scapulars (much worn then as a protection), prayer books – from large missals to colourful children's prayer books. Other stalls catered for bodily needs with tea, bread, buns, cakes, sweets, fruit, in fact anything one needed, giving the day a festive feeling. My family always walked home. Having fasted from midnight we did justice to rashers, sausages, eggs, puddings and golden fried bread: a meal fit for a king, my father said. Not a meal to be recommended today with such emphasis on healthy hearts. Some people spent the full day at Tobernalt, and I believe there were sports and music all afternoon. In later years we cycled back to the ball-alley near Tobernalt for dancing that evening. Having danced with gusto we still managed to cycle home in the velvety darkness of a midsummer night. So we truly celebrated Garland Sunday in Christian and pagan fashion as our ancestors had done before us.

Tobernalt is a special place for Sligo people and I have no doubt that it will continue to be so. Having retained its aura of mystique and history since time immemorial, it has become a restful corner in our hectic world. It is a place to stand still, to listen to birdsong and to the gentle gurgle of the stream on its way to the lake. It is to realise that thousands of men and women - now long gone and forgotten – have done this before us, bringing their worries and woes with them. We too will go and, like them, be forgotten while Tobernalt, with its ageless beauty and peace, will offer these qualities to anyone who seeks them, in this shady, tranquil place by the shores of Lough Gill.

WINTER, A MEMORY

Winter evenings, black, black nights
Memories of rooms lit by firelight,
Streets of flickering gaslight, dim shadows between
Spooky enough to make one scream.

Homes lit by lamp, gas and oil,
Candlesticks in every hall,
Snow on the ground and on branches bare,
Were leaves and fruit once really there?

Mufflers, gloves, coats, hats kept warm,
Bodies, fingers, toes whate'er the storm.
Youngsters longing for snow to stick
Of sleighs or slides then take their pick.

Dashing uphill, dragging sleighs,
Shouting, laughing, sliding all the way
Cold and frosty, winter wonderland
Better by far than sea and sand.

Angelus bells ring out in the dark,
Time for home, tea round the hearth
Crumpets toasted golden brown
Made teatime special in my old town.